The Quoting Heart

The Quoting Heart

a book of inspiring and encouraging words for everyday living

Roseanne Venturino

ISBN: 150308020X
ISBN 13: 9781503080201

Author's Note

■ ■ ■

The images shown for each month of The Quoting Heart were actual heart sightings in daily living.

January

January 1

▪ ▪ ▪

When you keep your destiny in mind, every minute of your day can become an opportunity to move closer to it.

When you're clear about the goals you've set out for yourself, you'll find signs all around you that pertain to them. Stay aware and follow your intuitive inner voice.
It's there to guide you.

Mission: Today, take one small action towards your vision to help it materialize. Stay aware of all the signs that come your way.

January 2

■ ■ ■

Never stop trying. There will be times in your life that you'll hit road blocks. It's up to you to find a new avenue, a different direction, a better way. Just steer clear of the dead end.

Each of us needs encouragement. Sometimes things just aren't going to go your way no matter how much you try. Don't give up, there's always another road that may bring you to a better place and a brighter tomorrow.

Mission: Learn to use your inner strength and creativity to make things work for you. No matter what life throws at you, there's a way around it. Change your perspective and listen to your heart for the answers.

January 3

■ ■ ■

Everyone has something to overcome and everyone handles things differently. Challenges are put before you to help strengthen you and teach you. Learning from these experiences is the key to strength and wisdom.

Everything you go through in life has a specific lesson for you to learn. When I was diagnosed with cancer, I realized that life can change in a second. You should learn to roll with the punches. It's not always easy but you have to remember that what doesn't kill you will definitely make you a stronger human being. The lessons you're taught through each experience will prepare you for the next one.

Mission: Learn to play the game of life. Those that do are happy and cheerful. They live in the moment. Let go of playing the victim and choose to be victorious.

January 4

▪ ▪ ▪

Nothing lasts forever. There will be times you'll have the world on your shoulders and times you'll have the world at your feet, neither is constant.

Change is inevitable. No matter how much you long for things to stay the same, it's not possible. Change doesn't necessarily signify something bad, just different. Newness is good for the soul.

Mission: Learn to ride the wave. Some days all will go well and other days may take a little more effort. Try not to attach yourself to either way. Take everything in stride.

January 5

■ ■ ■

The best gift you can give of yourself is your understanding.

People want to be understood, not judged. Too many people are misunderstood for their actions. You never know what burdens they may be carrying.

Mission: An understanding heart can truly help someone in their time of turmoil. Walk in someone's shoes for a moment. Place yourself in their situation to try and see things as they do.

January 6

▪ ▪ ▪

Feeling as though all your efforts were done in vain can be sabotaging your belief in your dreams. Realize that it's when you keep believing in yourself that your dreams will remain alive.

Belief in oneself is the key to success. Everything you want for yourself begins and ends with YOU. Never give up and never stop believing. You have what it takes to get where you want to be. Say it and believe it!

Mission: Things may not happen overnight but don't get discouraged. Everything worthwhile takes time and belief in oneself to come to fruition. Take some time to go inward to find your purpose.

January 7

■ ■ ■

Balancing your life requires you to go within. When you are centered and balanced you will stay calm and present in each moment without thinking of the next thing.

Life can be hectic at times. It requires balance in order to find contentment. Learning to stay present is imperative. You cannot enjoy life if you're always rushing from one thing to the next.

Mission: Take the time to live in the moment. Your life is your time. Take the time to enjoy it. The key to keeping calm and centered is to stay in the moment, accept things that cannot be changed, forgive past hurts, and exercise both mind and body daily.

January 8

■ ■ ■

Situations can be risky, but it's still worth taking chances. You may think you know it all, though there's still more to learn. Life seems difficult at times, but no one said it would be easy. You may think you've achieved perfection, but there's always room for improvement.

Life is about growth. If you choose not to learn, then you're limiting yourself from what you could become. You were created for greatness. Unleash your spirit to become all you can be. Don't settle for ordinary when you can be extraordinary!

Mission: Don't back down from opportunities that arise. There's so much knowledge out there. Think of every challenge you face as a stepping stone towards your success. Learn from it all and apply it!

January 9

■ ■ ■

We all want our lives to have meaning. Work on things that are important to you and need your attention. Take inventory of your life and learn to see and feel what truly matters.

Living with a purpose is crucial to your well -being. Everyone has a gift to contribute to society. Some of us find it early on, if we're lucky, others find it later in life, or not at all. Living a purpose filled life will give your life more meaning. Be conscious of your purpose. It's never a waste of time.

Mission: Find your purpose by paying attention to what makes your spirit come alive.

January 10

▪ ▪ ▪

Live the life you've always imagined and don't take NO for an answer. Never settle for anything less than you deserve and never let anyone deter you from your dreams.

Just because you've heard the word "no" too many times doesn't mean you're always going to hear it.

Mission: You have what it takes to make all your dreams come true no matter what anyone else may say. Keep trying for a "Yes". Opportunity is everywhere, you just need to find it. Be patient.

January 11

▪ ▪ ▪

When you put expectations onto others, you are setting yourself up for disappointment.

There's nothing better than relying on yourself to get things done. Your life is your own and it's best to make your own decisions. Stay in control and focus on what you need to do for you. Be your own leader.

Mission: Lower your expectations of others. Do not expect the world from anyone, it's not their place to give it to you. Expect more of yourself and you will become more content.

January 12

▪ ▪ ▪

The capacity to love and be loved is a gift. Never take it for granted. It can build you up, give you strength, and give your life purpose.

Everyone is in search of love and everyone needs it to feel lifted and strong. Love is powerful. It is a blessing. It can change the world. Begin by loving yourself, then you can love others.

Mission: *Love is the answer to all things. Be generous with it and accept it graciously from others.*

January 13

■ ■ ■

The best things in life are free. When you realize this truth, the struggle to have more will be less of a burden.

It's not always easy to see what's important. We need to realize that what's right there in front of us may be all that we need. We must stop accumulating things that we think will bring us happiness. This will never happen.

Mission: *Enjoy your family, friends, your free time, and nature. Realize these simple things are the things that truly matter.*

January 14

▪ ▪ ▪

Give to others the things you want for yourself and the fulfillment of satisfaction will be yours.

We get what we give as the saying goes. Help others along their journey by helping them reach their goals. Whenever we help others, we are inadvertently helping ourselves.

Mission: The universe gives you back those things you give away. Give something you want to others and it will come back to you multiplied.

January 15

▪ ▪ ▪

Seeing the glass as half full takes strength and a good attitude. Living your life this way will certainly bring the best to any negative situation.

It's not always easy to look at the bright side, but you should know that there will be a light at the end. It's there, though you can't see it right now. Darkness doesn't stay dark forever. The light is on the other side. Believe it's there and keep walking towards it. You will get there.

Mission: *Always remember that a positive attitude helps you to stay ahead of the game. The universe (God) conspires with your feelings to help you along. Keep looking up!*

January 16

▪ ▪ ▪

Each day there are new situations to face. We need to realize the strength we hold within to overcome all obstacles. It is there within us, even through our toughest challenges.

The challenges of life are tests of our strength. You are much stronger than you realize. You have the power to conquer anything that comes your way. Whatever the mind believes, the body will follow.

Mission: Never lose hope. You have everything you need inside of you. Never doubt that power within. Trust it and let it work for you.

January 17

■ ■ ■

People that are respected usually have something to be respected for. They have integrity and are accomplished individuals. It shows how far you've come when those respected are respecting you.

Reach for the stars and don't settle for less than you deserve. Live with the uniqueness that you were born with. Your gifts are your assets, don't let them go unnoticed. Share them with the world.

Mission: Make it a point to use your gifts and talents. Live your life earning the respect of those who are respected. Aspire to be someone who earns respect.

January 18

■ ■ ■

Never set limits on yourself. Life is game of challenges and you're ready to conquer each one.

You are capable of so much more than you realize. Some days we may not feel that we're good enough. Re-train your brain to believe you are always good enough and always ready to be your best.

Mission: Consider your life a game. Strive to be your best player in that game. Mediocre doesn't win.

January 19

■ ■ ■

It's all about the journey. As you take each small step, learn from these new experiences, and stay focused on the goal. This is when the destination begins to arrive without notice.

When you have a passion for what you do, it doesn't feel like work. Stay present and keep doing what you love. You will eventually be where you're supposed to be. Your purpose will unravel.

Mission: Your destination becomes the journey and vice versa. Be aware of every step along the way, and enjoy it.

January 20

■ ■ ■

May each new day be bright with a guiding light that leads the way. May it bring hope that all will be well. May it bring peace to bring you a sense of calm. May it bring love because that's what you deserve.

Keep meditation and prayer in your days. This is what will help you maintain centeredness and balance.

Mission: Have faith that each new day will be better than the last. Keep your faith and always live with hope and love in your heart.

January 21

■ ■ ■

Don't let your habits take control of your life. Stay focused on the things that are important to you. Bad habits can take over your mind and eventually your life, leaving you feeling like a different person.

Don't let yourself be controlled by anything. Bad habits will affect your character and weigh you down, eventually changing you as a person. They will become your worst distraction and they will take away living in the present moment. Letting your habits take over your life will leave you feeling out of control and defeated.

Mission: Learn to walk away from your bad habits. Stay in control of your life.

January 22

■ ■ ■

Life is about living, enjoying, and loving everything that brings joy to your heart. When you feel your best, you'll give your best to others.

Welcome each new day by being grateful. Honor all those things in your life that bring you joy. When you take the time to think about all the things to be grateful for, you'll be starting your day on a positive note.

Mission: Live your life with enthusiasm and confidence. Keep doing whatever it is that makes you feel your best self.

January 23

▪ ▪ ▪

You matter to someone, whether you're aware of it or not. Make sure your words and actions are positive. You can make a difference!

Never doubt your effect on another. The people you surround yourself with each day, whether it be your children, coworkers, relatives, and friends, are listening to you. Your words and actions may mean more to them than you know.

Mission: Be seen, be heard, be counted. Even when you feel like you don't matter, your presence, your words or just your way, can help make a difference in someone's life.

January 24

■ ■ ■

There comes a time in your life when you'll feel the need to hold on tightly to all that you love, not realizing that this is the time to loosen up the grip. That is how those things will remain.

Human nature makes us feel the need to grasp tightly to all that we need in life. Our ego is fear based and can push us to act desperately in situations where the opposite reaction is necessary. The tighter the grip on something, the more fear based it becomes.

Mission: *Choose to let go of things that you feel the need to keep close. You can remain close but not attached. It's unhealthy to attach yourself to anything. All things in life are temporary.*

January 25

■ ■ ■

Believe in having abundance and you won't fear lack. Believe in having success and you won't fear failure. Believe in possessing strength and you won't fear weakness. Believe in yourself and you'll always be led to where you're supposed to be.

The word BELIEVE has always been very meaningful to me. It holds a lot of power. I've never lost my faith or belief in God, no matter how difficult my life had become. Always believe things will work out for the best. No matter how bleak a situation may look, continue to believe that goodness is on its way.

Mission: There is power in believing. Believe in all things that serve you well and you will make it through any difficulty.

January 26

▪ ▪ ▪

If you want respect, don't belittle others. If you want help, offer it to others. If you want love, live with your heart open. Whatever it is that you want and need will come back to you.

Live each day with the thought of giving whatever you've got to others. Lift them up, fill them with hope, and show love freely. There's no reason to withhold all that you feel in a day. The world needs more giving people.

Mission: Offer something to someone who cannot repay you. Give more but expect less. Be grateful for the power of giving.

January 27

■ ■ ■

Anger and resentment imprison a person. Forgiveness is the key that sets you free.

It's impossible to live happily carrying anger and resentment in your heart. It will weigh you down like an anchor. Forgiveness brings freedom to your heart and mind. You deserve to be free.

Mission: When you are angry and resentful towards someone, they'll have a hold on you. You are only hurting yourself by holding onto it. Choose to let go and set your spirit free.

January 28

■ ■ ■

The wise man knows, believes, and trusts in his own heart. He is aware of the signs that others would consider to be mere coincidences.

Every day there are signs in front of us that we simply ignore. Signs from above that remind us that we're loved and protected. These signs come in all forms. One example may be continually running into someone from your past after not having seen each other in years. Maybe there's a message for you to receive from them or vice versa. Nothing is a coincidence.

Mission: A coincidence is God's way of hinting to us that we should pay attention to something in one way or another. Pay close attention to your next "coincidence".

January 29

■ ■ ■

Each of us has a fate, a reason for being, and a place where we should be in the world. Determination towards your goals is what you need to put forth. That's when the force of the universe will open the way.

One small action each day is all you need to reach your goals. It takes more than just a thought. Never stop reaching for what you want in life, begin with baby steps. Everything you want for yourself is attainable.

Mission: When you are confident in yourself and you have a plan, it's important to get that plan in motion. Take the first step towards that goal. You need to take action when you have a vision. Self- confidence, vision, plan, and action. You will get there!

January 30

■ ■ ■

Savor the love, beauty, and goodness that comes into your life and release all the hatred, ugliness, and unhealthiness that may linger.

Holding on to good thoughts and feelings will bring more things into your life that make you feel those good feelings. What you think about, you attract. Like attracts like. Keep those unhealthy thoughts to a minimum. Think and do those things that make you feel happy.

Mission: Take in every bit of goodness and beauty that you encounter throughout your day, and cherish it. Remember, your state of mind dictates your life.

January 31

■ ■ ■

The grass is not always greener on the other side. In fact, I'll be happy to stay here on the hard concrete.

Just because things may look perfect on the outside doesn't mean things ARE perfect on the inside. Looks can be deceiving. Don't get caught up in wishing you had someone else's life. Remember, everyone has something to overcome. Some people just hide it better than others. Each person has his own journey.

Mission: Learn to appreciate your life and whatever comes with it. Realize that everyone has something to overcome.

February

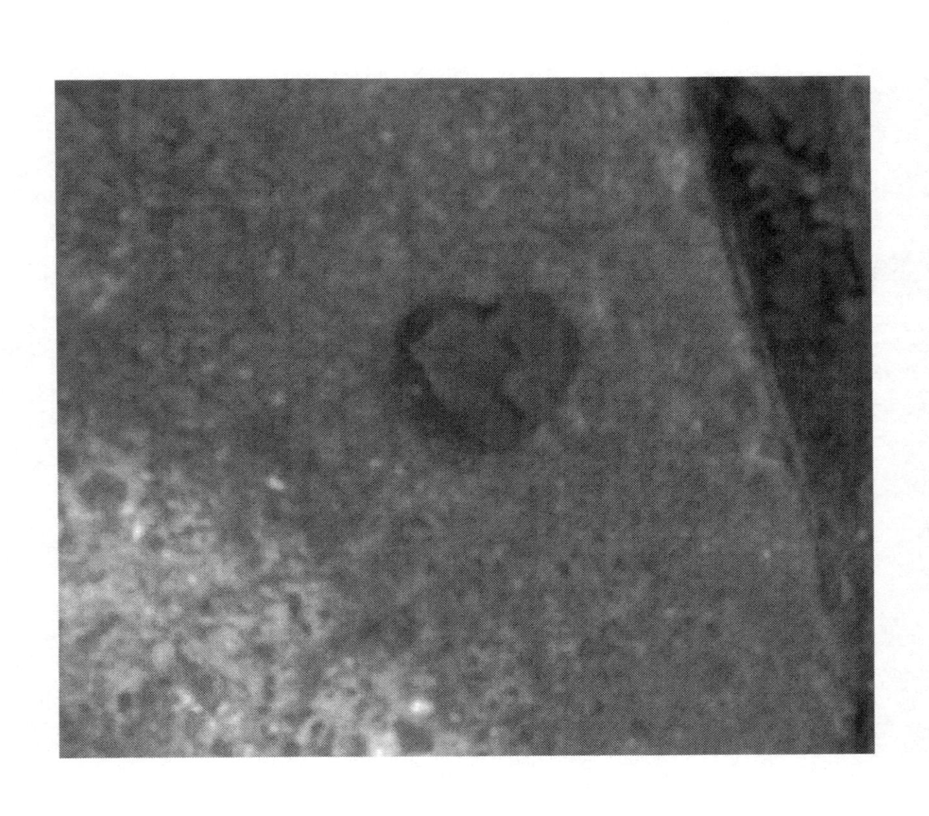

February 1

■ ■ ■

Don't let life get the best of you, give your best to life!

Life is full of ups and downs. Don't let the downs bring you down. Keep a positive attitude no matter what life brings your way. Be grateful for everything you receive, good or bad. It's all a lesson.

Mission: You were meant to give your all. Let your talents and gifts be known to all whom you encounter. Don't waste them, let them lead you to your highest heights.

February 2

■ ■ ■

Let go of all things that keep you stagnant. Open your mind and reach for better things. You are worthy of so much more.

When you settle for things, you're shortchanging yourself. Not everyone will tell you just how talented you are. YOU must believe that you are. You can do anything you set your mind to, so prove it to yourself.

Mission: Clear the clutter of your mind to clear a path for your goals. Too many times we get stuck doing the things that bring us a lack of fulfillment. Re-structure your thoughts. Put them in order so that you may begin to live your purpose.

February 3

■ ■ ■

It's important to keep the child alive in you every day. When you look at life through the eyes of a child, you will see the magic and feel the joy.

Children hold the secret to living in the moment. They are completely enveloped in their playtime. This is how joy sets in. They use their imagination well as they are perfectly content living in the moment without a care.

Mission: Children are innocent; they see the world untarnished. Learn from them to love life, learn from them to see the goodness and beauty in everything. Live childlike, it's great for the soul!

February 4

■ ■ ■

Be accountable for your own life. Don't expect others to make everything right. Stay on course and always be your own leader.

You can't place blame on others for the things that have gone wrong in your life. All your successes and failures come down to your own decision making. Expecting others to fix your mistakes will never happen. You are the captain of your own ship.

Mission: Your decisions ultimately lead to your fate. Learn to rely on yourself.
Take some time to think about important decisions, weigh them. Write down all the pros and cons.

February 5

■ ■ ■

Be mindful of your actions because everything you do affects someone else in some way.

Sometimes we make decisions for ourselves that affect those around us. When we ignore this fact, we can hurt others without realizing it. It can cause much pain and discomfort to them. The next time you're faced with decision making, consider all those that are involved.

Mission: Make a point to be aware of your actions. Be aware of who is involved in the circumstance before making your next decision.

February 6

■ ■ ■

You cannot re-create the past but you CAN create your future. You have the power to achieve everything your heart desires. There's no room for doubt. It's a belief in yourself that makes all things possible.

Self-belief is powerful. When you believe in yourself, you can move mountains. Don't let a little setback discourage you. Keep working through it and believe that you can do anything you set your mind to do. Giving up should never be an option.

Mission: Set your mind on your future goals. The past is gone. Get in gear for a bright future filled with promise. Always believe there's something great about to happen.

February 7

▪ ▪ ▪

It's when you stop giving that you begin lacking.

You were meant to be a giver. Giving is the greatest feeling in the world. Giving does not necessarily mean of monetary items. Be a giver of good vibes and positive actions. A giver should always give something that someone else needs, even a listening ear.

Mission: Live your life as a giver. Its benefits are nourishing to your soul as it lifts others' spirits. Giving is a true blessing to both giver and taker. You will always be blessed with abundance when you decide to become a giver.

February 8

■ ■ ■

Sometimes you just need to begin again. Starting over isn't a negative action if it's done with good energy and focus. It shows a sense of perseverance.

There are going to be things in your life that you'll want to do over, the right way. There's nothing wrong in beginning again. If there's a goal in front of you that you're working towards, then do your best in getting it the way you want it. Give it all you've got. This may mean starting over.

Mission: Learn to correct certain situations in your life that need fixing. Everyone needs to do this at one time or another.

February 9

■ ■ ■

Life is a competition with yourself to get better, stronger, and wiser.

Everything you encounter in life brings you to another level. Whether it's successes or failures, you're learning and growing. Stop comparing yourself to others and just keep looking for ways to better yourself. This usually takes getting out of your comfort zone.

Mission: *Look at the person in the mirror, that's your competition. Work on it each day.*

February 10

■ ■ ■

Untapped potential is like having all the knowledge in the world but only using what you need for your job. There's so much more to you.

Setting limitations on yourself is taking away your power. Many times, we keep ourselves limited because we're afraid to shine too brightly, or afraid that we may seem full of ourselves, or that we're bragging because we think we're so great. Well, guess what? You are great and there is greatness within everyone. Your job is to bring it out in the open.

Mission: You are capable of so much more than you think. Don't doubt your greatness, own it!

February 11

■ ■ ■

Karma will never leave you lonely, it always comes back around.

Good energy as well as bad energy acts as a boomerang. Make a point to keep your energy positive. You get what you give.

Mission: Be careful what you do to others because life has a way of returning the favor. Always emit good energy.

February 12

▪ ▪ ▪

Don't give up because you haven't gotten where you want to be. You're probably closer than you think!

Many times, people want to quit just as they're approaching their goal, not realizing just how close they are. Sometimes the road to our goals gets tough. Don't get discouraged, keep persevering, and keep moving forward with your dreams. Anything you can imagine in your mind is attainable in your life.

Mission: *Do not give up when the going gets tough. Realize you just need to hold on a little longer. Take time to enjoy the journey.*

February 13

■ ■ ■

Your greatest source of power is your intuition.

Everyone has intuition or an "inner voice". Some choose to ignore it, as others seem to live by it. This inner voice is not meant to be ignored. It is your guide.

Mission: Take the time to listen to that "gut" feeling. It holds the truth to many of life's dilemmas.

February 14

▪ ▪ ▪

Whether you're two, forty -two, seventy -five or ninety-five, you will always have the desire for love and care, companionship and freedom, comfort and security, and a life that's worth living.

Some values in life will never change, regardless of age. Those values have special meaning to you and they are a part of living a wonderfully fulfilled life. Never deny yourself or your loved ones of those things that are important for a rich and meaningful life.

Mission: Be sure to care for all your loved ones of every age. Show them how much they mean to you as often as possible.

February 15

■ ■ ■

Hard work always pays off in some way, shape or form. Never feel that your efforts are done in vain. Nothing worthwhile comes easy.

Hard work builds character. The hard work you put in today will pay off tomorrow. It is better to put your all into something than to not have tried at all. Everything you do with all your effort will not be wasted. It will serve you well eventually.

Mission: Don't hold back. It's important to put your all in everything you do, especially if it means a lot to you. Continue to work on the goals you've set out for yourself. Your day will come.

February 16

▪ ▪ ▪

Choose your friends, your words, and your arguments, wisely.

Be selective with those you call friend, not everyone is going to be on your side, but you can still be kind, weigh your words, and keep peace.

Words cannot be taken back easily; they can scar someone emotionally. There's no need to argue about everything, there's a lot of negative energy in arguing. Sometimes we may feel the need to speak up when something is important to us, but there's always a way to keep peace.

Mission: Promote peace. All your choices affect your life and your well- being. Choose positive minded friends, positive words, and limit your arguments. Re-examine the situation before participating in an argument. Most times it's not worth the fight.

February 17

■ ■ ■

Actions speak louder than words but sometimes unsaid words speak the loudest.

If there is something that needs to be said to someone, don't hold back. Speak your mind to others, especially those that need to hear it the most. Words can be comforting when spoken at the right time.

Mission: *Show sensitivity and be sure to know when and when not to say something. You can hurt someone's feelings by holding back what needs to be heard.*

February 18

▪ ▪ ▪

The things that we push away from our life may be just the things we need.

We all have times in our life that are full of confusion, self -doubt, anxiety, and uncertainty. Those times you may find yourself to be extremely vulnerable. Stay aware of the things or people that may be depleting your energy. Also, stay aware of those things or people that may give you great energy and reassurance. Sometimes, during our low points in life, we tend to hold on to anger and push away the right things and people.

Mission: *Many times, we push away the things we think we don't need. Living in fear can sometimes prompt poor choices. Choose to live with love in your heart. Take a step back, enjoy some quiet time, and go within to realize what you need for a life fulfilled.*

February 19

■ ■ ■

Sometimes you just have to do whatever it is that gets you through.

Life isn't always easy, though it's still a blessing. It's up to you to see it as just that. Find whatever it is that brightens up your day. It could be a walk in the park, a great movie, or simply hanging out with a good friend. Whatever brings a smile to your face and joy to your heart is a blessing.

Mission: *Find the small things that bring you happiness and incorporate them into your day.*

February 20

■ ■ ■

Be daringly original. Originality is a personal gift, be true to it!

You were born to be a unique individual. Don't hide all your amazing-ness. Others will appreciate what you have and will want to hang around you. Never feel embarrassed or ashamed of who you are. Be real and live your life authentically.

Mission: Share your God given talents. Your purpose in life is to share your gifts.

February 21

■ ■ ■

Stop doubting yourself. Whenever you doubt your actions and capabilities, you set limits on yourself. Remember, your spirit is unlimited and should be free to soar.

Self- doubt is like punishment to your soul. Many times, we place limitations on ourselves and our abilities. Having faith in your own ability takes time, and we've all been there. You don't have to begin something by being great, but you can become great by beginning something. Practice makes perfect.

Mission: *Everyone at some point feels "not good enough". Retrain your brain by practicing positive affirmations daily for a stronger self-esteem.*

February 22

▪ ▪ ▪

What you see may not always be what you get. This can lead to making mistakes. Learn to fine tune your inner sense. It can save you from lessons to be learned.

Let your intuition be your guide, that's what it's there for. If something feels uncomfortable, it's probably going to become a problem. The more you know the less you'll need to find out.

Mission: Ignorance is not always bliss. Find out the facts before you jump into any situation. When things look too good to be true, that's when they usually are.

February 23

■ ■ ■

Happiness is not a destination, it's a state of mind. Learning to be happy with everything you have in life right now is the key to getting there. There is so much to be grateful for, and that is where happiness lies.

Instead of waking up and complaining about everything going on in your life, get used to appreciating everything you have in your life. During my cancer journey, I was grateful that I could keep working and doing what I loved to do. I was able to continue exercising; I was able to instruct fitness classes and personal training. I continued writing positive quotes daily. These are the things that make me happy and I felt so blessed to continue. I felt blessed that I could still be me.

Mission: Keep a journal of things to be grateful for and refer to it daily.
Write down five things every day in your journal that you're grateful for. Before you know it, you'll see the glass as half full. Make a habit of feeling thankful for all your blessings.

February 24

■ ■ ■

To attain success, big or small, you need to accept responsibility for your actions. Blaming others for your mistakes will only cause you to live in the past. Success of any kind only happens when you keep moving forward.

Learn from the past, but don't carry it with you. Mistakes will be made along the way but they shouldn't be the same ones repeatedly. A part of being successful is to have some failure along the way with lessons well learned.

Mission: Keep in mind that the road to success is attained by staying focused on your goals, expecting more of yourself than from anyone else, and choosing to never give up.

February 25

■ ■ ■

Today, be grateful for the things you never thought you'd have.

There comes a point in your life when you would never have thought you'd have what you have now. Be grateful for that. During your lifetime, you've overcome many obstacles and had the tenacity to keep moving forward to get what you wanted. It most likely didn't come easy.

Mission: *Think back to the days you didn't have the many things you do now. Write them down, reflect on them and be thankful for what is to come.*

February 26

▪ ▪ ▪

If you want the difficult things to become easy, then believe they are easy. If you tell yourself you can't do something, then you're probably right!

Sometimes you must trick your mind into believing you can do even the most difficult of tasks. Instead of telling yourself that you can't do those things, tell yourself that you can do anything. Your mind is a powerful tool. Use it to serve you well.

Mission: *Try changing your inner dialogue. Catch your thoughts before they become negative. Your mind is your greatest tool. Whatever you believe about yourself will be.*

February 27

■ ■ ■

Don't get used to being a taker. Takers aren't grateful. The giver knows there are those less fortunate. He knows to be thankful for life's smallest blessings.

Life consists of takers and givers. The takers may leave you feeling depleted as the giver is the lifter of the spirit. It's important to realize which kind of people you surround yourself with. Are they takers or givers? Also, are you a taker or a giver? The givers are usually the happier people.

Mission: *Live with a giving heart. Become more aware of others' needs. It will make your life more meaningful.*

February 28

■ ■ ■

Release the heaviness in your heart. Bring peace to the world in the way that you know how. One person can contribute to that change. Be that person.

In a hectic world, inner peace can take some time to achieve. It takes much practice but it can be done with daily prayer, meditation, and centeredness.

Mission: Practice those things that bring peace to your mind and spirit. Then help others to do the same.

March

March 1

■ ■ ■

Each of us needs a place. A private place that's all our own. A sanctuary that fills us with peace.

Peace doesn't always come easy so it's important to find it. Everyone has the capacity to find peace and be a peacemaker for others.

Mission: *Create a place in your house, garden, or a space within your mind that brings you peace and quiet. Whether it be an actual place, a mindset, or simply doing something that's a healthy escape for you. Practice going there when life gets out of control. This can be your private sanctuary, your sacred place.*

March 2

■ ■ ■

You can't always be someone for everyone, just make sure everyone respects the someone that you ARE.

Make a point to be yourself every day. It's easy to fall into the trap of people pleasing, but that will never lead you to a happy life. If others aren't happy with the way you are, it's none of your business. Just move on.

Mission: *You deserve respect no matter who you are or what you do. Expect it from others and do the same in return.*

March 3

■ ■ ■

Creativity is the essence of life. Let your creative side flourish into all areas. It's something personal, only you can offer. It's your gift to share.

You are blessed with many skills and gifts. Being creative is one of them. Many people live day to day hiding their creativity, never realizing it can be of great help or value to someone else. Whether it's artwork, fashion, decorating, writing or anything that may come naturally to you, let it be known.

Mission: *Be grateful that you are unique with a special gift. A gift that's different and all your own. Let it be known to all those who come your way.*

March 4

■ ■ ■

Whenever you feel the need to be other than yourself in someone's presence, that is a sign that you are somewhere that you shouldn't be.

Having to put on a front to appeal to someone else is clearly giving you a sign that something's wrong with the situation. Be yourself regardless of the situation, or keep walking.

Mission: *Be true to yourself in every situation and with everyone you encounter. Have faith that it's the right thing to do at all times.*

March 5

▪ ▪ ▪

During your lifetime, there are many incidences that you'll need to experience as each one prepares you for the next. Coincidences are not just chance happenings. They are a part of the ultimate plan for you.

There are coincidences, or God winks, that happen all around you each day. It's up to you to notice them and understand the underlying message. There's always something the universe (God) is doing behind the scenes for your sake.

Mission: *Begin taking notice of all the signs that appear in your life unexpectedly. Realize that they're there. Ask the universe (God) to send you signs of reassurance when in doubt.*

March 6

■ ■ ■

Adversity is the building block of character. It can be like a strong force. It can hold you back from all you've set out to do. It can tear away all that you've worked for and all you've meant to become. It can also help you realize what you're made of.

Having obstacles in your way can be either a good or bad thing. It's all in the way you handle issues when they get challenging. You can see them as either a challenge to overcome or a challenge that's overbearing.

Mission: *Try seeing each challenge as something good for you. Let the next challenge change you into a better person. Learn to see the positive in the negative.*

March 7

■ ■ ■

Everything else becomes irrelevant once you realize what's truly relevant.

It can take some time to realize what's important in your life. It may take some trials and errors. Once you've become aware of the important things, hold on to them. Do whatever it takes to keep them in your life. Then you can eliminate all the irrelevance, as it serves no purpose.

Mission: Sometimes you'll need to hit a low in your life to realize what's important. Keep a journal of all those things that matter to you. Don't take anything for granted.

March 8

■ ■ ■

A life without balance is like a main avenue without traffic lights.

Balance is the key to having a life that flows well. Be sure to balance your life by giving each area of it the proper time and attention, making moderation a priority.

Mission: Take time to give every area of your life proper attention. Make a point to stay presently in the moment with each.

March 9

■ ■ ■

You have the power to be limitless. Don't let self- doubt hold the reigns.

You were born to be fearless, courageous, and unlimited. Sometimes other people's views can interfere with your way of thinking. Comparing yourself with others doesn't mean you are "less than". The doubter will continue to doubt until he has enough confidence in himself to believe otherwise.

Mission: *Work on your self- confidence every day. You are so capable of attaining all your goals. Tell yourself this each day. Believe in yourself and your goals and take small steps towards them daily. You will receive what you wish for if you're diligent. Your mind is your power.*

March 10

■ ■ ■

Simplify your life. Clear away the clutter. The less stuff around you, the clearer you'll become within. It's a direct effect!

A life with less stuff makes it easier to invite the right stuff in. Whether you have clutter in your space or clutter in your mind, let it go.

Mission: Rid your space of too much stuff. This includes your brain. After all, our brain runs our day and creates our life.

March 11

■ ■ ■

Change is inevitable. It shouldn't be feared, but welcomed.

Life will allow for many changes to come your way. It should be an expected part of your journey through life.

Mission: *All challenges in life bring changes. The word challenge holds the word change in it. Learn to accept changes gracefully. There can be a new-found excitement when you accept change into your life.*

March 12

■ ■ ■

Everyone has their story and everyone has their own path in life. The lessons you've learned along the way have helped shape your attitude and helped develop your character. You've earned your worth.

Loving oneself is something everyone should set as a goal. You have to be with yourself all through your days, months, and years. You might as well learn to be comfortable with your own company on your journey.

Mission: Don't look for the approval of others to validate your self-worth. Only you know where you've been and where you are now.

March 13

■ ■ ■

Find something in each day that brings happiness to you, however small.

Everyone has something that makes them happy. Sometimes just reading a good book or watching a funny movie can fill you with a sense of contentment.

Mission: It's the small things in life that are so precious and meaningful. Find joy in them. Learn to appreciate what's in front of you.

March 14

▪ ▪ ▪

Don't get too caught up in worldly possessions. It's great to have nice things to appreciate, but not to worship.

There may be times that you'll tend to focus too much on owning expensive things, thinking they will bring happiness, or make your life seem more impressive. You keep accumulating one pricey thing after the next until you've come to the realization that material things cannot bring lasting happiness. True happiness is priceless.

Mission: Don't get obsessed with monetary things. Don't expect to take the material things with you either. Remember, they are only quick fixes.

March 15

▪ ▪ ▪

If you want answers, then ask questions. It's not a sign of ignorance, but of intelligence.

Don't be afraid or embarrassed to ask questions. Think of life as a school. You're here to learn as much as you can. Stop worrying about being judged or ridiculed. It's important to keep learning and growing. Knowledge is power.

Mission: *Life is full of unanswered questions. It's up to you to keep asking. The more, the better.*

March 16

■ ■ ■

A successful person finds motivation through his passion, joy through his work, and contentment through his heart.

Everyone defines success differently. But if one thing is true, it's realizing your passion in life and making a living with that passion. It would seem like never having to work a day in your life.

Mission: *It's important to find your purpose to feel complete and balanced. Look within, it holds all the answers.*

March 17

■ ■ ■

Once you stop allowing your ego to rule, you'll stop inviting trouble into your life.

The trouble that comes into your life is usually prompted by the ego. It can rule your life if you let it. It always wants to be in charge and it doesn't know when to quit.

Mission: *Learn to recognize when the ego takes over. If it's not something positive or good for all, then it's usually ego based. The ego loves trouble. It is based on fear, not love.*

March 18

■ ■ ■

Always imagine yourself to be better off than you are. After all, what you think about, you become.

Aspiring to become better should be something every one of us should consider daily. It's important to see yourself enveloping traits and habits that will ultimately mold you into a better person.

Mission: *You can become anything you set your mind to. Even if you haven't gotten to where you want to be, don't give up. Instead, imagine you've already accomplished your goal. This is one step towards how you will receive it.*

March 19

■ ■ ■

Live your life being the exception to the rules.

It's important not to limit yourself or put yourself into a one size fits all box. You were born to be exceptional. Never doubt all the gifts and talents that you possess.

Mission: *Keep reaching for the stars. Don't live your life settling for ordinary. You have what it takes to be extraordinary.*

March 20

■ ■ ■

If you keep surrendering to your weaknesses, you'll always feel as if you're starting over and you'll never know just how strong you can be.

Being strong usually means having to dig deep. It's not always easy. Sometimes you may need a little help if you want your life to take a different direction. You'll have to let go of some things from your past. Those things may be certain habits, ways or addictions that keep you in the same place.

Mission: *You are much stronger than you think. Train your mind to overcome the obstacles that come your way. Stop living in a vicious circle. Put yourself where you want to be.*

March 21

▪ ▪ ▪

Every thought you think today brings an action that affects tomorrow.

Your thoughts as well as your imagination are real. Whatever you can envision in your mind, you can achieve in your life. Pay attention to your thoughts, they predict your future.

Mission: *Choose your thoughts carefully, as they lead to actions. Your thoughts direct you to your future.*

March 22

▪ ▪ ▪

Don't expect from others what you can't expect from yourself.

High expectations are the key to disappointment. If you cannot depend on yourself to do something, do not expect anyone else to make it happen for you.

Mission: *Knowing and trusting yourself is the foundation for inner peace. Self -reliance in life is a gift to yourself. Lower your expectations of others and increase them for yourself.*

March 23

■ ■ ■

Remain humble in a world full of materialism. Don't let material possessions dominate your life. You empower the things you worship.

It's great to have nice things as long as you don't worship them. Remembering what's truly important in your life is what brings contentment. Look at the material things as mere accessories that have very minimal effect in the end.

Mission: *Material possessions only help to satisfy you temporarily. They can never bring true happiness. Stay grounded and realize the best things in life are free.*

March 24

▪ ▪ ▪

Greed is not the way that leads to having more money, it's the way that leads to having less of a heart.

Sometimes having more is not the answer to becoming rich. When your character is compromised, it usually isn't worth it.

Mission: Always wanting something more is not good for your spirit. Learn to want what you already have and help those less fortunate. This is the way to contentment and gratification.

March 25

■ ■ ■

Let the desire to be something better be the fuel in your engine every day.

It's important to hold yourself to a certain standard and to keep your dreams alive. You have the power to become whatever your heart desires.

Mission: Your passion gives you energy. Let it lead the way to a better, more fulfilled life.

March 26

▪ ▪ ▪

Every situation's closure, every heartache you've experienced, every person whose left their impression upon you, every bit of victory you've earned, or defeat you've endured, was meant to be. It was meant to prepare you for the new path that awaits you.

Everything that happens in your life is meant to happen at that time. Experience is your greatest teacher.

Mission: *Everything you experience in life is meant to prepare you for something that hasn't yet occurred. Pay attention to every experience and learn from each one.*

March 27

■ ■ ■

If you don't set limits on yourself then don't let others set them for you.

Never let another person run your life for you. Your freedom is your personal gift to do as you please.

Mission: Your potential is without limits. Believe in yourself and never give up, regardless of what others might say.

March 28

▪ ▪ ▪

You can only be who you are, only give what you have, only teach what you know. Your possibilities are endless when you continue to learn and grow.

Never stop learning and growing. Educate yourself throughout your entire life. You will find life to be much more interesting and satisfying as you keep learning with each new day.

Mission: Never stop learning. Read something new every day, take a class, learn a second language. Education is a gift to yourself.

March 29

■ ■ ■

Never let your head get so filled with yourself that your heart is left empty for everyone else.

Live your life with an open heart. Your life becomes meaningless when you are self -consumed. You were born to live and give.

Mission: Self- centeredness leaves you in a lonely world. Choose to focus your attention onto others.

March 30

■ ■ ■

Whatever it is that you want for yourself, give away to another. Watch how it comes back to you tenfold.

The universe has a funny way of conspiring to make things happen for you when you want something. Just as the universe gives unto you, so shall you give to the world.

Mission: The more you give out the more you'll receive. Make a point each day with the intention to give to another.

March 31

▪ ▪ ▪

Discomfort leads to growth, whether it's mental or physical.

Whenever you feel challenged, you are facing a change. Get used to the discomfort, just move with it. There's usually an opportunity coming right along if you can learn to roll with it.

Mission: *You need to step out of your comfort zone to experience change. Unfamiliar territory is a good thing for your mind and spirit. Do something that scares you today!*

April

April 1

■ ■ ■

The simplest words and gestures have the most profound meaning.

Sometimes it's better to keep things simple. It's safe to say that everyone understands simplicity. That is what makes it so meaningful and powerful.

Mission: *There's no need to speak eloquently or do extraordinary things when it comes to expressing yourself from the heart. Keep your words and actions simple and filled with meaning.*

April 2

■ ■ ■

There's an upside and a downside to everything. If you focus more on the upside, the downside will fade away.

Focus on positivity. All things, even the seemingly bad ones, have a positive point. At first it may be hard to find, but it's there, or it will eventually come to be.

Mission: In every situation, you have a choice. You can focus on the positives or the negatives. Choose to focus on the positives and more good things will flow your way.

April 3

■ ■ ■

Never let yesterday's mistakes be your obstacle for tomorrow's greatness.

You cannot keep dwelling on your past. Continue to move forward in the direction of your dreams. Your past mistakes are a part of your future's greatness.

Mission: Don't dwell on things that don't serve you well. Rid your mind of the mistakes of yesterday. Focus on all the positive goals you want to bring to your life.

April 4

■ ■ ■

Determination, patience, and courage are the only things necessary to improve any situation.

If you want to see changes, you must put in the work. You can change any situation you're confronted with. You need to be determined enough to want those changes, learn patience for things that need time, and be courageous enough to never give up.

Mission: *Stay on track, don't deter. A positive, diligent mindset is crucial for change.*

April 5

■ ■ ■

Learn to be a good listener, you never know when you'll be inspired.

Life isn't all about you and the world certainly doesn't revolve around you either. Sometimes the most important of all senses is hearing. Not just hearing words, but truly listening.

Mission: *Work on your listening skills. They are important for learning anything new, and the key to opening new ideas and insights. They can be the perfect means for changing your life.*

April 6

▪ ▪ ▪

Only in silence can we hear our own truth.

Turning off the noisy mind chatter is crucial to becoming in tune with yourself. Find a soothing, quiet place in your day to unwind. This is the place you will truly get to know yourself.

Mission: Be sure to take some quiet time for yourself daily. Meditate, pray, and go within. Learn to know and love yourself. It will make your life easier. When you learn to trust in who you are, you will never have to rely on anyone to make your world a better place.

April 7

■ ■ ■

You should not have to depend on the praise of others to realize your own self- worth.

Life is tough and can wear you down if you let it. Trying hard to attain the praise of others should never be the way. Don't fall into the people pleasing category in order to feel worthy. You'll need to go through many experiences to help you realize your own strength, and this is how you will come to know your worth.

Mission: There's no need to try to please everyone in your life, as this is never going to be. Don't waste your energy in trying too hard to gain the praise of everyone. If they like you, you'll feel it, if not, that's none of your business.

April 8

■ ■ ■

Empathy, kindness, and love for others begins with an authentic self.

You cannot possibly feel for others if you don't care about yourself. You can try to fake it, but eventually it will show. You must let those feelings come from within your core in order to affect another. Superficiality doesn't go far.

Mission: *To become your authentic self, you must get rid of the ego, live in the moment, and stop pretending to be someone you're not. Stay aware of where your feelings are coming from.*

April 9

■ ■ ■

The sooner we realize that we are all connected, the easier it will be to understand each other.

We are more alike than different. If we could consider the people of the world as brothers or sisters, we would show more mercy and forgiveness towards each other. It would make it easier to get along, and we'd stop judgment of each other. We were put on earth to be teachers for one another.

Mission: *Each one of us is connected to another in the universe. We are like a woven pattern, intertwined. When we hurt others, we are hurting ourselves overall. Be a peacemaker.*

April 10

■ ■ ■

Your attitude can either hinder your spirit or help it to soar.

Attitude is everything, so adjust it accordingly. Having a positive attitude can make you exceptional on many levels. It can help any given situation to become an opportunity. Your perception is key to living a wonderful life.

Mission: Wake up each morning thinking one positive thought at a time. Watch how your life unfolds for the better.

April 11

■ ■ ■

Never lose the passion in your heart, never lose sight of your dreams, and always live with a sense of purpose.

Your passions make life worth living. It's important to figure out those things that bring joy to your heart, then make them work for you to live your best life. Without dreams, your life will seem unenthusiastic.

Mission: Find whatever it is that makes you want to jump out of bed in the morning. Let it guide you. It will satisfy your heart, mind, and soul.

April 12

▪ ▪ ▪

Follow your own light to your own destiny.

You cannot follow someone else's path and expect to reach your destiny. Listen to your inner voice daily. Stay true to yourself and you will get to where you belong.

Mission: Begin each day saying "I will". I will accomplish what I've set out to do. I will become someone. I will become whom I am meant to be.

April 13

■ ■ ■

Lying to others will only reveal the truth about yourself.

When you live your life being untrue to others, you are only fooling yourself. Lies will always be revealed in one way or another. It is always best to be honest, than to have a lying heart.

Mission: Keep yourself honest. Good character comes with honesty first. Let others earn their trust in you.

April 14

■ ■ ■

You have mastered the gift of giving when you've learned to be a giver and expect nothing in return.

Life is better when you've learned to give without receiving. It can do wonders for your spirit. Stay aware of others who are in need of your gifts.

Mission: Begin to give to others without expecting anything in return. The best gifts are given when nothing is given back. It's the best feeling in the world to be a giver. Today, give something to someone who cannot repay you.

April 15

■ ■ ■

You will never attain true happiness if you hang on to jealousy, anger, resentment, and bitterness.

If you let your ego lead the way, you will never be a happy person. The ego carries around past resentments. It makes sure things done to you aren't forgotten or forgiven. It doesn't know how to let go.

Mission: *Clear your mind of all negative feelings. Let them go, they are not the path to happiness. They will imprison you if you choose to hold on. Choose the higher road. Let go of those things that do not serve you well.*

April 16

■ ■ ■

Never doubt your worth. Everyone is valuable to someone.

Have you ever stopped to realize how important you may be to someone? There are many people in the world who can use your presence around them. You can have a positive effect on someone every day by sharing your unique gifts. Never hesitate to share the gifts that you've been born with to help encourage another person in some way.

Mission: You are important in this world. You are productive. You have assets to offer the world and you are powerful. Use your gifts and talents, don't waste them. Be someone that another looks up to and aspires to become.

April 17

■ ■ ■

The soul that lives humbly cries out for peace and love. The soul that lives by the ego cries out for attention.

To keep a humble heart, you need to remember where you came from. No matter how intelligent you are, no matter how well you do things, no matter how wealthy you may be, learn to treat everyone the same.

Mission: Choose to be a peaceful, loving person. The world needs more peacemakers, there are too many horn blowers out there. You, alone, can change the world.

April 18

▪ ▪ ▪

Your destiny will unfold when there is certainty in your heart.

Once you know what you want to do, you'll find where you belong. The key is to finding whatever it is that you want.

Mission: If you have a set goal, put your all into it. Be diligent, be confident and never give up.

April 19

■ ■ ■

All things that are important to you should bring you a sense of joy, gratitude, and fulfillment. If they don't, re-think what's important.

Joy, gratitude, and fulfillment should be a staple in everyone's life. When you can honestly say that you've found these, you will always have hope for any situation which may arise.

Mission: *Every now and then it's a good thing to re-evaluate the things you feel are important. Make sure those things are not bringing you down, corrupting you, or causing you stress.*

April 20

■ ■ ■

The key to achieving happiness is surrounding yourself with goodness. Fill your life with people who genuinely care about you and have a positive effect on your life. Be aware of the wolf in sheep's clothing.

During your lifetime, friends and acquaintances will come and go. The ones that stick around not only for the good times, but the bad times too, are the ones to call keepers.

Mission: Keep goodness close. Be choosy with friends and trust in God. Ask Him to lead the way.

April 21

■ ■ ■

There is something in each of us that is considered a gift. Acknowledge the power you have from this gift. Don't boast or brag about it. Instead, use it as a source of inspiration for others.

You were born with certain gifts to offer. These are different from your traits. These gifts can help others in some way. Never waste them.

Mission: Find your talents and gifts. Offer them to others who could use some inspiration. Help make someone's world a better place.

April 22

▪ ▪ ▪

It's not always easy to be the best you can be every day. We all have days when we feel sad, hopeless, discouraged and bitter. We're only human.

No matter how you're feeling or what's going on in your life, always try to do your best. When you bring your best self to every situation, the situation will always be better.

Mission: *The best thing to do when these feelings overcome you is to change the direction of your thoughts. Focus on what's right in your life and what brings you peace and contentment. Then do the things that bring those results.*

April 23

■ ■ ■

Life won't always treat you fairly. Once you accept this fact, you can roll with it better.

Life will have many twists and turns. You should expect the unexpected. The only thing in life that you can control is your attitude towards the unfairness.

Mission: *No matter what life throws your way, stay level headed and positive. Keep your chin up and keep on forging ahead.*

April 24

▪ ▪ ▪

Having courage is an important trait. It takes courage to be your true self every day, it takes courage to forgive, it takes courage to live out your dreams. Most importantly, it takes courage to never give up.

Living courageously takes practice. Start with small things until it becomes a daily habit to live this way. Having courage does not mean you're unafraid. It means you're afraid but you're still following through with what must be done.

Mission: *A courageous spirit sets you free. Find the courage in your heart to do something you thought you could never do. Break free from the chains that hold you back and start living courageously!*

April 25

■ ■ ■

There are times in your life that you may feel you've loved in vain. But keep in mind that having the capacity to show love from your heart is a gift that's never wasted.

You should never hold back what you feel if you want to keep things real. Every kind of relationship works better when you show what you're feeling. It's when you feel that you can't express yourself the way you'd like to that things begin to turn sour.

Mission: Share your love. Love is the ultimate healer; it can change lives.

April 26

■ ■ ■

Your destiny should not be left in someone else's hands. You have one life; get it the way you want it!

Self -reliance is key to getting things the way you want them. Never let another make decisions for you. You are capable of more than you realize. Stay in charge of you.

Mission: Take control of your life. It's up to you to find the right direction. It's up to you to pave your own way. You have the power to make it great on your own terms, just trust yourself.

April 27

■ ■ ■

Sometimes we just need to absorb the stillness of the moment to remember who we are, what we are feeling, and what we desire.

When it's your time to re-charge, you'll need to shut the world out. Never feel guilty for time spent alone, it's necessary.

Mission: *Don't feel that you always need to be caught up with the noise and chatter of life just because you think you should be. Learn to be still and enjoy the quiet time.*

April 28

■ ■ ■

Never let time become your enemy. Cherish it, enjoy moments in it, and acknowledge it. Time is precious, try not to waste it.

All we have is time. The most important time is the present. This is where time is most enjoyed. Practice staying in the moment and continue to make memories.

Mission: *Learn to use your time wisely. You aren't going to be here forever. Do what you want to do and be who you want to be. Do as much as you can while you're here. Make time work for you.*

April 29

■ ■ ■

Not everything in life is difficult. Sometimes we just make it that way.

There are so many times that we make things more difficult than they need to be, instead of just seeing the situation as it is. Life was not meant to be complicated. People tend to think things should be a certain way, and this is what complicates matters.

Mission: *Learn to see things just as they are. Appreciate the simplicity.*

April 30

■ ■ ■

Life is about progressing to the next level while maintaining balance.

It's important to keep moving forward, but be careful not to take on too much. You don't want to overload yourself to the point where everything becomes out of order. Set limits as you progress.

Mission: When balance is thrown off, don't regress, just go at a slower pace.

May

May 1

■ ■ ■

Live your life under your own terms. Live courageously, passionately, and purposefully. Live with abundance in your heart.

Your life is your own. You were meant to be here for a reason. Don't settle for anything less than you deserve.

Mission: *Expect abundance in all areas of your life. Your positive attitude coupled with your feelings of wanting to share abundance, will help bring many blessings to you and to those you care about.*

May 2

■ ■ ■

With change, there is growth. Never let fear be the obstacle.

Welcome change into your life. Moving out of your comfort zone is the best thing you can do for yourself. It helps build character and helps you to realize all you're made of. Never be afraid to keep progressing, and always take things to the next level.

Mission: *We are empowered with every new beginning. If something scares you, do it anyway!*

May 3

■ ■ ■

Walk in faith and you'll never walk alone. Your darkest moments will eventually have a brighter outlook. Your tears of sadness will turn into tears of joy. Your love and passion for life will soon return.

Never doubt there's light at the end of the tunnel. When I was eighteen years old, I had gone through a bout of depression. I began to make poor choices. My mind was filled with uncertainty for the future. I was feeling lost. I had premonitions of my mother getting sick and dying. I never thought I would see the light again. I used to see people laughing and being lighthearted, and I would ask myself, "Could I ever be that way again?" But with daily prayers to our Lord, and the love from others, I made it through. You may not see the light right away, but keep walking through the darkness. The light is there. I promise you it is there. You will be stronger when you get through it.

Mission: *Never lose faith as miracles happen every day. Keep believing that all things are possible. Your faith is your salvation.*

May 4

■ ■ ■

Life is a beautiful place when you know how to care for yourself and surround yourself with all the things that bring you joy.

Make a point to nurture yourself. Only you know how to take care of yourself. Only you know what makes you happy. Only you know what brings you peace and contentment. Give these gifts to yourself every day.

Mission: Be sure to never let go of what brings you peace and contentment. It can be the simplest of things that do the most good.

May 5

■ ■ ■

Every circumstance has a positive point. Sometimes it's just not seen.

Many times, when negative things happen, we can't see a positive side. We can't help but think that we are doomed and there's no way out. This cannot be further from the truth. Every single situation will eventually show a bright side. Keep your faith and know in your heart that this situation too, shall pass and you'll be a better person for it.

Mission: *Learn to believe in positivity. Each circumstance, whether good or bad, that presents itself, is an opportunity for something better. Look for the greater good in all of life's turning points.*

May 6

▪ ▪ ▪

To each his own. When someone doesn't act as you do or live their life in a conventional way, rather than belittle them, be inspired by them. It takes more courage NOT to be like everyone else.

Live and let live. Try understanding others rather than frowning upon them. Everyone was made to be different. The world would be a boring, stagnant place if everyone was the same.

Mission: Today, accept someone as they are without ridicule. Every person is unique. Try to learn something from them.

May 7

■ ■ ■

Each of us is born with a particular gift or talent. When you don't use these blessings, you are limiting your potential to become your best self.

You were born to shine. The gifts and talents you possess were meant to be shared. Your talents are what make you stand out, they are empowering. These are the things that make life worth living. Never let a day go by without using them.

Mission: Become aware of your gifts and talents by noticing the things that "wake up" your spirit. These are your passions in life. Act upon these.

May 8

■ ■ ■

Life's challenges come in all sizes. The next time you are faced with one, try to perceive it as a stepping stone rather than a wrecking ball.

Challenges are put before you to help you become stronger and wiser. You are stronger than any obstacle that comes in your way. God will only give you what you can handle.

Mission: *Life will always be full of challenges. Learn to deal with them gracefully. Each challenge brings you to a stronger, more empowered YOU. Use them to change for the better.*

May 9

▪ ▪ ▪

There are many things in life that hold a sense of wonder. Keep your heart open and eager to venture into that wonderland.

Never let yourself stop learning and growing. Every day there is something new to learn if you keep your mind open. This is what will bring you a sense of fulfillment.

Mission: Don't hesitate to try new things and explore new adventures. See the world through the eyes of a child.

May 10

■ ■ ■

Don't go through life unchallenged or too safe. It's important to take risks and put yourself in uncomfortable situations to feed your spirit and grow your mind.

Sometimes the very thing you need is to get uncomfortable. This is the growth that needs to occur for you to progress to the next level. Make it a point to get out of your comfort zone regularly. You are capable of much more than you realize.

Mission: *Try to do the same old things, differently. This will build the confidence and courage to try new things. Be brave!*

May 11

▪ ▪ ▪

Once you've learned to master your thoughts and feelings, your life will become magical.

Being in control of yourself and your thoughts is priceless. Your thoughts and feelings are a large part of how your life unfolds. Train your mind to think positive thoughts every day. Eventually, with daily practice, you will find positives in every negative situation.

Mission: Your thoughts and feelings create your reality. Begin today thinking one positive thought. Tomorrow, do the same, and so on.

May 12

■ ■ ■

The most important thing to adjust every day is your attitude. It can make the day as bright as the sun or as dark as a black cloud.

Everyone has something to be grateful for. When you feel grateful, the universe will deliver more things that keep you feeling grateful. When you're feeling ungrateful, the universe will deliver more things to keep you feeling ungrateful. The right perception is what matters. You choose.

Mission: Begin your day with a grateful heart. It's going to be a great day!

May 13

■ ■ ■

Everyone has the ability to attract what they want into their life. You must become aware of the power that you hold. Once you become aware, you will never lack anything.

Whatever you want for yourself will come to be if you carry good feelings about it. Never get discouraged, there is always hope for a brighter day, brighter tomorrow and brighter future. Just as the ocean is full of abundance so is your life.

Mission: *The universe is abundant and you can bring abundance into your life just by acknowledging that you deserve abundance. There is no reason to lack anything. Envision having it, take a step towards it, then believe that it's on its way.*

May 14

■ ■ ■

Doubting your worth hinders your potential. The way you perceive yourself has a great effect on how far you will go.

Having self-confidence is crucial for success. Work on your confidence daily by doing things that are unfamiliar to you. Be eager to learn new things to become a more well-rounded person. The more you know, the further you'll go.

Mission: Practice confidence. Look in the mirror each day and tell yourself that you are worthy of all good things. Train your mind every day with positive affirmations.

May 15

▪ ▪ ▪

Never assume what another is thinking. Many things happen in the hours of the day that could affect someone's mindset.

You'll never fully understand what goes on in someone else's mind, so stop guessing. Everyone has their life to live and their own challenges to face. It's easy to assume but usually the assumption is incorrect. If you care to know what's going on with someone, just ask them. Communication is the key for maintaining healthy relationships.

Mission: Today, give someone the benefit of the doubt before you assume or criticize. Don't be afraid to ask questions when something doesn't feel right.

May 16

▪ ▪ ▪

Many things will never be understood and many things cannot be explained. One thing is for certain, ignoring difficulties doesn't solve the problem. You need to face them to erase them.

The best way to face any obstacle is head on. Accept whatever is going on in your life. Acceptance of things, especially obstacles, makes them easier to overcome.

Mission: *You don't have to have everything figured out, but you do have to face your problems. Learn to accept your problems, then you can begin to take the necessary steps towards rising above them. One thing at a time.*

May 17

■ ■ ■

We weren't meant to be perfect, just perfectly meant to be.

Every one of us has a purpose, a reason for being. We may make mistakes along the way, but if we've learned and grown from them, they were worth making. Our mistakes will only make us wiser.

Mission: Accept yourself with your flaws. There will always be room for improvement. No one is perfect, and that's ok.

May 18

■ ■ ■

The best person to come to know is yourself.

You have to live with yourself daily. You might as well become best friends. You are truly blessed when you can be happy with yourself. Only you will know how you truly feel about everything.

Mission: *Learn to get comfortable in your own company. You will always have YOU for your entire lifetime. Get used to relying on yourself. Become your own best friend. When you are comfortable being alone, then you can be comfortable with anyone.*

May 19

▪ ▪ ▪

Your future is unfolding every day, so be sure to keep your sights set on where you're going.

Your life becomes what you put into it. Stay focused on where you want to go. Set goals, then act upon them. One small step each day will get you there.

Mission: Envisioning your goals is the first step to attaining them. Create a vision board of all the things you hope to accomplish. Refer to it daily to help keep you on track.

May 20

■ ■ ■

The way you feel about your life will determine how you live it.

Your attitude is crucial for living a quality life. The right attitude will lead you to good things, the wrong attitude will lead you to bad things. It's that simple!

Mission: Practice feeling grateful today and every day. Your life is a gift. Steer clear of bad habits, keep goodness in your life and always think positively.

May 21

■ ■ ■

Perseverance is the spirit's unwillingness to quit, the unwavering mindset that's never willing to settle. It's that inner voice that screams, "I'm not done yet!"

If you want to achieve your dreams, it's important to keep them in mind every day. Dreams do not just happen; they must be worked towards. This in turn, develops character. If you want something in life, go and get it. Never give up on your dreams.

Mission: Today, think about what it is that you want from life. To be successful at something, you need to give it your all. If you want something badly enough, let it be the one thing that becomes your daily focus. Keep believing, and don't ever give up.

May 22

■ ■ ■

Success tastes that much sweeter when it's mixed with a little failure.

Failure is part of success. When you learn to accept failure along the way, it will be easier for you to continue towards success.

Mission: Mistakes are a part of success. Look at a mistake as a stepping stone. Find a way to let it work in your favor. Once you've attained your goal, you will be glad to have learned from your experiences, both good and bad.

May 23

■ ■ ■

No act of kindness, however small, goes unnoticed, is forgotten, or will ever be done in vain.

Don't be afraid to be kind to others. They will only love you for it. The world needs more kindheartedness. If it doesn't seem appreciated, do it anyway. It will always make you feel good in the long run.

Mission: Do something kind for someone today, while seeking nothing in return. Kindness is never wasted energy.

May 24

■ ■ ■

Time is the keeper of all answers.

Time reveals the truth about everything. Have patience for those things you can't find answers for. Have faith that time will tell. It's just another reason time is precious.

Mission: Don't rush your time, learn to live in every moment of it. Eventually it will reveal all you need to know.

May 25

■ ■ ■

Whatever makes you happy sets you free!

Be sure to include enjoyable things in your day. Let those things that you love to do be your reward. Take care of your responsibilities first, but leave some time to do whatever makes you happiest.

Mission: Keep your inner child alive in your daily life. Do one thing every day that makes you feel like a kid again.

May 26

■ ■ ■

There will be times in your life that you should stay quiet and times you should be heard. Times that you should stay timid and times you should be bold. They'll be times that you should stay and times you should walk away.

It's important to know when to act on things and when not to. Listening to your intuition is always helpful, though many choose to ignore it. Your inner voice is sometimes the best thing to listen to when it comes to uncertainty. Next time you're at a crossroads, stop and listen. Let it guide you.

Mission: *Practice listening to your intuition. You can do this by meditating or by sitting quietly. It will guide you in your difficult decision making times.*

May 27

▪ ▪ ▪

Don't get too far ahead of yourself, you may forget where you've been. Don't get left too far behind, you may forget where you're going.

Stay on a steady pace with your life. Be sure to stay focused on the here and now, the present moment. Don't let your mind wander off to the past or future. None of that is relevant now.

Mission: Try to stay level in everything you do, and keep moving at a steady pace towards accomplishing your goals. Remember, slow and steady wins the race.

May 28

■ ■ ■

Everything you care about needs constant nurturing. Don't neglect what's important in your life. Nothing lasts forever.

When you care about things, you are attentive to them. That's what keeps them remaining in your life.

Mission: Show the special people in your life how much you care for them. Show appreciation for the things that give your life meaning.

May 29

■ ■ ■

Sometimes we may lose our way, sometimes we know exactly where we're going, and sometimes we are already at our destination without knowing it.

There are different phases in our life that leave us with different feelings. Realizing every phase is important in becoming who we are meant to be is something that should be reflected on. Each phase, even those times that we're feeling lost, is meant to happen.

Mission: *Pay attention while on your journey through life. Take action to make things go your way. See it in your mind and believe it in your heart as each moment unfolds your destiny.*

May 30

■ ■ ■

LOVE is the most powerful, yet gentlest, the most difficult, yet simplest, the most abundant, yet lacking, the most sincere form of expression, yet so misunderstood.

Love is the solution to many problems. It can save a life, it can turn a negative situation to a positive, it can heal. Love carries a lot of power. It needs to be given and taken.

Mission: The power of love is immeasurable. It's the cure for the heart broken and broken spirited. Give your love generously to others and watch your own world change.

May 31

■ ■ ■

Celebrate yourself for all that you DO, all that you ARE and all you've yet to BECOME.

You deserve to be celebrated. If you find that nobody cares to celebrate you, then celebrate yourself. Remember, you are worthy.

Mission: Give yourself a pat on the back today. Realize that you are a powerful spirit and deserving of all good things.

June

June 1

■ ■ ■

The way you see things makes all the difference in how you feel about your life. Perceiving your life as a game to be played helps you to see the lighter and brighter side of every challenge that comes your way.

If you change the way you look at things, the things you look at will change too.
It's not always easy to see things in a different way, but it's worth a try.

Mission: Look for the positives in every situation. They're always there. Change your outlook and change your life.

June 2

■ ■ ■

Listen to your intuition. It's there to help you, not hurt you. Just take the time to listen.

Your intuition will always help you. It's your inner guide, your saving grace, your navigator.

Mission: *You are blessed with an intuition. Pay attention to it, tap into it daily with quiet time, meditation, or prayer.*

June 3

■ ■ ■

Sometimes things get worse before they get better. Don't get discouraged. Remember, all things in life, whether good or bad, are temporary.

If everyone would realize that all things are temporary and nothing is constant, there would be less fear and sadness in the world. Whether things in life go right or wrong for you, stay grounded. Don't get too high or too low emotionally. This will help you deal better with disappointments. Accept things as they come, yet expect nothing.

Mission: Stay strong and positive and just keep walking. No matter what you're going through in your life, do not stop doing what you do. Continue to move through the discomfort. There IS a light at the end.

June 4

▪ ▪ ▪

Connect your hardships with growth and replace bitterness and blame with forgiveness.

Hardships can break you away from your comfort zone but that can be a good thing. It can help you grow as a person **as adversity** builds your character. Accept challenges with grace and reap the benefits of your effort put into them.

Mission: Beginning today, accept all that comes your way, good or bad. Don't complain about everything that doesn't go your way, it's all meant to teach you something.

June 5

■ ■ ■

Make the most of each moment. These moments become the memories of your past. Stay focused, and live through them. Do what you love to do with those whom you love.

The most important thing you can do each day is stay focused and present in the moment. Time goes by so fast, and we can never recapture a moment that's passed. Learn to live presently. Life will become more enjoyable.

Mission: Don't take one minute for granted. Life is short, so learn to live in the present moment to get the most out of the days of your life.

June 6

▪ ▪ ▪

Don't wish for someone else's life, no matter how good it looks. Most people have something to overcome. Learn to be happy with your own life, and stay grateful for everything you have, every day.

It seems everyone wants what they can't have, and the grass always looks greener on the other side. But usually that's not how it is. If every one of us can see the beauty that's in our lives, and realize how special the things and people that surround us each day truly are, then we wouldn't be feeling this way.

Mission: Stop taking things for granted. Learn to love your life and everything in it. Imagine how your life would be without those wonderful things. That's how you will learn to appreciate what you already have.

June 7

■ ■ ■

The dreams you keep in your heart and mind are there for a reason. They should never be smothered, taken lightly, or repressed.

Your dreams are meant to be expressed, unleashed and flourished, never having to be surrendered or given up. They should guide you, give you a reason to wake up in the morning and bring purpose to living.

Mission: Never stop believing in your dreams because with hard work and diligence, there will come a day that those dreams will become your life.

June 8

▪ ▪ ▪

Everything changes in time. Do not fear change. It can take you places you haven't been.

Sometimes the best thing that can happen to a person is change. Learn to walk along an unfamiliar path and welcome something different into your life. There's always another door opening as another one closes. Change can be empowering.

Mission: Learn to accept, rather than resist the newness of change. It can do you good!

June 9

■ ■ ■

Never underestimate the power of "alone time". It's important to become comfortable with the person you are. Once you know and understand yourself, it will become easier to know and understand others.

It's important to come to know yourself. The way to get to know yourself requires going within. Quiet time and meditation are great tools in getting to know what's truly in your heart.

Mission: Find some time today to go within. Listen to what your heart and mind are saying.

June 10

■ ■ ■

The world is filled with different kinds of people with different points of views. That's what makes it interesting.

Rather than condemn others for thinking differently than you, try to see their point of view, and learn something new.

Mission: Keep an open mind to others' views. Be open to new possibilities. Try to see life from a different perspective.

June 11

■ ■ ■

Whatever you worship, you empower. Be careful of those things you think deserve power, they may just leave you powerless.

Worshipping material things, inanimate objects, movie stars or other things that are considered fantasy, may leave you feeling inferior. Learn to honor and empower the person you are.

Mission: Be selective. Make sure the things you honor and love are worth your time and energy.

June 12

■ ■ ■

Wake up and feel blessed. You were put on this earth to reach higher heights. You weren't born to stay the same. With each new day, give yourself the chance to honor the person you are. Set your standards higher, dream bigger and make perseverence a part of your character.

You are a blessed person, from everything that you are to everything you've yet to become. Take on the challenges that bring you higher. Get yourself in gear for greater things. You are deserving of it all!

Mission: Go the extra mile today. If you're working on a project, take it to the next level. If you're not, challenge yourself to something new.

June 13

■ ■ ■

Instead of looking at failure as a step in the reverse direction, look at it as an experience which brings you closer to success.

It takes some failure to bring you to success, so don't get discouraged. Most failures help you to learn what you need to do to get where you're going. Get yourself back on track and keep moving forward regardless of your mistakes.

Mission: Reflect on your mistakes. Starting today, try looking at them as necessary steps along the way. Realize that they are part of the process to success.

June 14

▪ ▪ ▪

If it seems that you're waiting forever for things to go your way, then you need to get in motion and start living on purpose.

Things will not happen for us if we don't take action. Action is the tool for success. Live your life with your sights set on the goal. You'll get there. You'll never be that far from success as long as you don't give up.

Mission: Do one thing today that brings you a step closer to your goals.

June 15

■ ■ ■

Try not to take yourself too seriously. The universe is a loving and forgiving place, so give yourself some slack. After all, we weren't meant to be perfect.

You don't have to go through life so serious. Lighten up by letting things go. You don't need to carry the world on your shoulders.

Mission: Make a list of the things that cause you stress. Try seeing the lighter side of every situation you've listed.

June 16

▪ ▪ ▪

Your mind can be your worst enemy. Train it to be your best ally by thinking positive thoughts throughout the day.

Whenever you get caught up in your thoughts, they'll begin to control you. Next time you feel the need to over analyze a situation, consider all the unnecessary negative energy you are consuming. Train your brain to work with you, not against you.

Mission: Try replacing every negative thought with a positive one. Your life will change as your thoughts do.

June 17

■ ■ ■

Always keep a hunger for living the most beautiful life you've imagined.

A passion for living life to the fullest is essential for feeling fulfilled. Make the most of your days by doing the things you love to do with the people you care about. Don't shortchange yourself. The world is your oyster!

Mission: Live and love all that you can. You were put on earth to do just that. Live life to the fullest!

June 18

■ ■ ■

If you find that you are convincing yourself that something is right for you, then it's definitely wrong for you.

If you feel the need to keep telling yourself that something is right then by all means, it's wrong. The right things just feel right; the wrong things feel wrong. It's that simple.

Mission: *Stop ignoring the things that you know are wrong. Usually the hardest thing to do and the right thing to do are one in the same.*

June 19

■ ■ ■

You can make someone's day with just one sincere compliment. Never underestimate the power of words.

Don't hold back saying something nice to someone. Make someone feel happy by showing them some attention. Keep those around you lifted up, and remember that people may forget a lot of things, but they don't usually forget how someone made them feel.

Mission: Pay someone a sincere compliment today. It will lift their spirit as well as yours.

June 20

■ ■ ■

Sometimes your WILL can be more powerful than your knowledge. Nothing changes without the will to make it happen.

A strong will can take you far. A strong will doesn't settle for less than deserved. A strong will seizes the prize. Most importantly, a strong will never gives up.

Mission: Use your strong will to make things happen for yourself. Remember, where there's a will there will always be a way.

June 21

■ ■ ■

Everything is a process. From learning to growing, from seeing to doing and from becoming to being.

Anything worthwhile takes time. You can't expect things to fall into place in a day.
Everything takes time to flourish, but you need to put the time and energy into it.

Mission: Stop rushing the process. Things will unravel as they should once you have a plan. Then, put that plan into action.

June 22

▪ ▪ ▪

It's difficult to bring good things into your life if you don't believe that good things will happen. Expect good things to come your way. Make room for them in your life.

Consider yourself worthy of all things good. Invite them into your life. If you love yourself enough to welcome the good, in time, with the intention to have it, you will receive it.

Mission: Fix your mindset. Realize your worth, and learn to accept all the goodness you deserve.

June 23

■ ■ ■

The effort you put into your work is like the amount of gasoline you put into your car. It will take you as far as how much you put into it.

It's important to put your all into your goals. Slacking won't make things happen. Be diligent towards your goals and you will reach them sooner. Your determination is your fuel.

Mission: Take your work seriously. If you want to be good at anything, you need to give attention to it.

June 24

■ ■ ■

Don't live your life as a doubter. A doubter will never overcome his obstacles. A doubter will never realize his capabilities. A doubter will never put his trust in anything. A doubter will never come to know all the miracles a hopeful mind can bring.

Being a doubter will never lead to greatness. Anyone who has ever accomplished something great had *believed* that they could do it. Your entire perception on life will change the minute you change your way of thinking. Doubting is negative, while believing is positive.

Mission: Practice being a believer. You need to believe in a good life. You need to believe in yourself and your capabilities to have one.

June 25

■ ■ ■

It's important to take advice from others when you're in a dilemma, though it's more important to listen to yourself when it comes to making your final decision.

When you constantly listen to others' advice, you are not living to your true potential. You are more knowledgeable than you realize. Tap into your inner guide to help you on your way. You will be happier to know that your decision was your own. You may need to learn something from the consequences of that decision.

Mission: Begin listening to your inner voice to help you with decision making.

June 26

■ ■ ■

Live your life as your BEST self. These traits will help you attain your goals:
B- Brave
E- Energized
S- Strong
T- Tenacious

No matter what you are trying to achieve in life, be **brave** by facing it head on. Stay **energized** throughout the process by showing enthusiasm. Stay **strong** when things don't go your way, and remain **tenacious** regarding goals by not giving up

Mission: *Today, become the champion you see yourself being. Think champion thoughts, carry yourself like a champion and believe in yourself as a champion does.*

June 27

■ ■ ■

Everyone deserves to feel good about themselves. Don't withhold a compliment to another where credit is due. It doesn't make you any less of a person if you show praise to another.

When you show praise to others, it makes you feel better as a person. Those who withhold praise show their own insecurity. Holding back a good word doesn't make anything better.

Mission: Today, give someone the praise they deserve. Always give credit where it's due.

June 28

■ ■ ■

The things that bring you the most joy can also bring you the most sadness.

Life is about finding things you love and loving them to the fullest. It's never dangerous to love things with all your heart, that's what life is all about. Loving hard may bring you heart-ache at times, but it shows you've truly lived.

Mission: Don't hold back. Live and love all that you can in your one life.

June 29

■ ■ ■

Everything you see, every person you meet, and every experience you encounter, is there for a reason.

Everything happens for a reason and the universe helps to line up certain people, experiences, and events to help us along the way.

Mission: Everything you've experienced up to this point in your life is preparing you for something bigger. Believe that the universe is on your side.

June 30

■ ■ ■

It's important to keep a balance with whatever brings you peace, money, and love.

Peace, money, and love aren't always easy to come by, yet they are indeed necessary for living.

Mission: To achieve balance, you need to divide your time. Don't overwhelm yourself with any given situation. Stay level headed and avoid becoming obsessive.

July

July 1

■ ■ ■

Stop dreaming, start doing. The things you want aren't just magically going to fall into your lap.

The life you want can't just be imagined. You need to envision it, and feel it deep down in your soul as if it's already yours. Then take the necessary steps towards making it happen.

Mission: *Begin taking the necessary steps towards what you want out of life. Make it a part of your daily routine as though it's a necessity. Keep your focus on that one thing, and see it through.*

July 2

■ ■ ■

Live as if impossible doesn't exist. Learn to depend on the power within to attain all your desires.

You'll never know what you can accomplish if you haven't tried. Just as the word impossible has the words I'm possible in it, signifies that there is power within you. A power that's great enough to achieve most anything you desire.

Mission: Set your mind to achieving whatever you want, regardless of your current situation.

July 3

■ ■ ■

Everyone deserves happiness, and that includes you. A sudden change can open a whole new beginning for you.

Sometimes you can get caught up in your daily routine, yet in your heart you know there's a better way. When your life begins to feel mundane, that's the time to change something.

Mission: Today, do something out of the ordinary. Break up your usual routine. It doesn't have to be a major change, begin with something small. It could be as simple as changing your path home from work.

July 4

▪ ▪ ▪

Your past is the sculptor of your soul.

Each one of your experiences leaves an impression upon you and ultimately determines the kind of person you'll become. The way you handle each experience is what makes all the difference.

Mission: Always think twice before you act. Learn to see each experience as a building block of your character.

July 5

■ ■ ■

Your determination is your fuel, your desire, and your ability to design your own life. It's what sets you apart from the rest.

Determination is key to conquering your fears, obstacles, doubts, or anything that gets in your way of moving forward. It's the most important component to attaining success. Determination is your path to the finish line.

Mission: Don't let discouragement settle in. Listen to the passionate voice within that screams "no quitting allowed!"

July 6

▪ ▪ ▪

Never tell yourself that it can't be done. Instead, say confidently, "I'm doing this", "I've got this!"

Your words and beliefs about yourself are powerful. They can either bring you up or tear you down. They have a huge effect on how you feel about your life and your attempt at attaining anything you've ever dreamed about.

Mission: Be mindful of the things you tell yourself daily. Let go of the doubt and negativity. Practice substituting positive thoughts for any negatives.

July 7

▪ ▪ ▪

Until you know yourself, you'll never understand anyone else.

We were brought into this world alone and we will leave it the same way. Get to know yourself by spending time alone. There's no need to always have people around you for security. Become independent, it's the only way you'll ever truly come to know yourself.

Mission: Practice being comfortable in your own skin. This is how you'll learn to trust yourself. You will be an inspiration to others.

July 8

▪ ▪ ▪

Just because something comes easy to you doesn't mean it does for everyone. Everyone has something to learn from another.

Be proud of the gifts and talents that you have. There's nothing that can limit you more than unused talent. Someone, somewhere, needs your talents. You have been born with them for a reason.

Mission: Make a point to learn from someone every day. It's possible they can teach you things that can make your life easier. Do the same for them in return.

July 9

▪ ▪ ▪

Sometimes you should just let things take care of themselves.

Life will always present obstacles. It's the way you handle them that matters. Don't be so quick to try and fix things that are going wrong around you. Many times, situations can fix themselves. Believe and trust in God and yourself enough to know that everything will be all right.

Mission: Don't stress yourself out trying to solve everything. Let some time go by and think positively. Your attitude can make all the difference.

July 10

▪ ▪ ▪

You are the only one that is held accountable for making you happy.

Stop searching for the perfect job, person, or lifestyle thinking it will bring happiness. Happiness is not a destination or possession. True happiness comes when you can look at your life and be grateful for all that you have.

Mission: Today, count your blessings. There are so many things in your life to be grateful for. Write them down on paper daily. Celebrate all your blessings.

July 11

■ ■ ■

Never let someone else tell you what is right for you. Follow your own heart.

Life is full of decision making. Though it's a good idea to take advice, it's important to listen to what comes from your heart.

Mission: Trust yourself. Learn to make your own decisions. There's no need to depend on another to pave the way for you. You'll never have what you want if you don't think or speak up for yourself. It's your life, live it your way.

July 12

▪ ▪ ▪

Be serious about your work. Show the world what you're all about.

If you're lucky, you'll find your purpose early on in life. It makes all the difference when you live life on purpose. Your work will seem more relevant as a contributor to society.

Mission: You will earn the respect of others when you show them that you're serious about what you do. When you're serious about it, you'll put care into it; in turn, you'll be great at it.

July 13

■ ■ ■

Not everything that comes your way is meant to stay. Enjoy it while it's there, though it may not be a part of your destiny for the rest of your life.

Some things in life are just passing through. They may be there to teach you something you need to learn on your journey.

Mission: Take the time to enjoy and be grateful for all those things that bring you happiness.

July 14

■ ■ ■

Always remain grateful for life's blessings. Even more so for those in disguise.

There are signs of blessing everywhere. It's up to you to take notice of them. Live with an open heart. Feel good, feel God.

Mission: Life will always have a way of helping you out. Remember that you are blessed beyond measure.

July 15

■ ■ ■

You can't go through life being afraid of every outcome. Trust in yourself and let your faith carry you beyond your fears.

There will be times in your life that make you feel that there's no other way. Keep your faith. A change will happen soon enough. You are not what has happened to you.

Mission: Dare to take a chance on something. Without risk taking, you'll be stagnant. Live today as if it's your last.

July 16

▪ ▪ ▪

Each person you encounter will leave an impression on you. They will either teach you a lesson or learn one from you.

Your life is not intended to be lived in isolation. We are all connected and there is no person that you've met that you weren't supposed to meet.

Mission: *Be thankful for those people you've met along the way that have taught you a lesson, whether good or bad.*

July 17

▪ ▪ ▪

Without forgiveness, you will never be happy, whole or free.

When you are unforgiving, your heart is closed. When your heart is closed, you will not experience the many graces and blessings in life. You will continue to be a prisoner.

Mission: Today, open your heart and forgive someone who hurt you. Let go of bitterness.

July 18

■ ■ ■

You should never let your circumstances imprison you. Your life can turn a brighter way on any given day. Expect it!

Each day is a new day. Begin it with a brand-new way of thinking. Live with a knowing in your heart that things will always turn out for the best. Life is full of small miracles.

Mission: Where you are now is not your final destination. You need to believe that good things are on their way. Stay positive, and believe that you are deserving.

July 19

▪ ▪ ▪

No matter your age, your wealth or your wisdom, lessons will always be there to be learned.

There are lessons to be learned in everything you do. Don't doubt that a lesson can bring you wisdom. The best way to show you've learned from a lesson is to never repeat it.

Mission: Stay grateful for your lessons, they make you who you are.

July 20

■ ■ ■

The ego appears to be so strong and powerful, yet once it's let go, you'll realize it's just a lightweight weakling.

The ego always wants to be in charge. It's starved for attention. It's bold and it's all about itself. Wherever the ego is involved, there will be trouble.

Mission: Learn to recognize when the ego takes over and try to eliminate it. Remember too, the ego is fear based.

July 21

▪ ▪ ▪

Kindness is not stupidity; it's doing the right thing.

You should never second guess showing an act of kindness. It's never the wrong thing to do. It's something that's never done in vain. It serves well to everyone involved. We need more kindness in the world.

Mission: *Do something kind for someone today, especially someone who least expects it. It serves the receiver as well as the giver.*

July 22

▪ ▪ ▪

Becoming your best self won't happen without helping others to become theirs.

When you begin to help others to see their own gifts and talents, you are raising their spirit, giving them confidence, and helping them become their best self. In turn, your own spirit is lifted to its highest self.

Mission: Lift someone's spirit today. Let them know their best quality. Tell them how they have affected you.

July 23

▪ ▪ ▪

Everyone has something to think about, be sure to keep it positive. Everyone has something to learn about, learn something that betters yourself. Everyone has something to talk about, speak kindly. Everyone has something to forget about, choose to forget your regrets.

Because we're human, we have things in common. Many of us have a thought pattern that is harmful to our spirit and our lives. Our thought pattern is helping to form our future. Our mindset is powerful. It's the most important adjustment to make in our daily living.

Mission: *Today, decide to think good thoughts. Set up your future with thoughts and actions that will bring you further in life. Leave the past behind.*

July 24

■ ■ ■

Everything falls into place once you have faith, inner strength, and patience.

Having faith, inner strength and patience doesn't come easily. Sometimes life's struggles can teach these. Faith to know that things will get better, inner strength to carry the burden, and patience throughout to realize it's not forever. Anything good takes time.

Mission: Take the time to center yourself. Stop wishing everything would happen for you NOW.

July 25

▪ ▪ ▪

Love is timeless, it will always remain. It may take a different form, though it always finds a way.

To love and be loved is crucial for your well- being. Love is eternal. Even when we leave this world, love remains.

Mission: Let someone know you love them today. Show them through your actions that you care.

July 26

■ ■ ■

Do something just for you today. Some days you just need to make yourself happy.

It's important to nurture yourself and contribute to your own well- being. It's not selfish, it's necessary.

Mission: Be good to yourself. Love, honor, and respect yourself. Let go of the things that bring you down.

July 27

▪ ▪ ▪

Never let the fear of failure get in your way of trying something different. There's no better way to reach higher heights than to get out of your comfort zone. Whether you succeed at it or not, it's worth the attempt. Either way builds character.

Don't be afraid of newness, it can change your life. Opportunity doesn't knock every day, so take the chance on the next one that comes your way.

Mission: Try something you've never done before just to see how it feels. Each time you try something new, you'll be that much stronger and confident because of it.

July 28

▪ ▪ ▪

Consistency in your work, your behavior, and your actions, is what earns trust from others.

It's important to show consistency in all that you do. It's what lets others know that you can be reliable and counted on. If you want others to trust you, then be consistent.

Mission: Try to become the kind of person that people can depend upon. Earn the trust of others. A good character is a consistent one.

July 29

■ ■ ■

You're only meant to do what you can do. Remember, what you can do is without limits and beyond what you think.

Once your mind believes that you can do something, the body will follow.

Mission: Learn to trust in yourself by relying on you. Believe that you have the power and the ability to do anything. Create the reality you desire.

July 30

▪ ▪ ▪

It seems everyone is searching for something. Most people think once we have attained that particular something, then we will be happy.

Searching for the perfect life, perfect person, or perfect job will never happen. Life itself is imperfect, so are we. Learning to have the perfect attitude is the best way to deal with all the imperfections.

Mission: *Stop searching for perfection, instead, learn to deal with the imperfections within yourself and within your life. Accept the things that cannot be changed. Adjust your attitude and be grateful for what you have.*

July 31

▪ ▪ ▪

When you have the ability to love and be loved, then you will always have plenty.

Love makes the world go around. It's what life is all about. When you have the capacity to love others and live with an open heart, you will be blessed.

Mission: Always keep your heart open no matter what you're currently feeling. Having love in your heart to share with others will always keep abundance flowing into your life.

August

August 1

■ ■ ■

Learning to take care of yourself is your responsibility, no one else's. Keeping yourself happy is a large part of staying healthy.

Never take your health for granted. All through my life I was healthy. I ate right and exercised just about every day. Then, unexpectedly, the sneaky, silent disease of cancer threatened my life. I'm doing alright these days, though cancer still poses a threat to my life. I have learned to live in the present moment every day. I remind myself that I still have me. I still have so much to be grateful for.

Mission: Never take your health for granted Keep yourself healthy in mind, body, and spirit on a regular basis. Do something, however small, for yourself each day that makes you smile and brings happiness to your heart. Life is short.

August 2

▪ ▪ ▪

Keys to a happy life... Live in the moment, appreciate the small joys, keep abundance in your heart and stay grateful.

Happiness is not found in a most flamboyant lifestyle. It's found in the simplest of things. It's not a place, it's found in your heart and mind.

Mission: Practice these 4 things daily until it becomes second nature to you and watch how your attitude and your life begins to change.

August 3

■ ■ ■

Making the most of what you have is how you need to live regardless of your current situation.

Every day is a gift. Whether you have everything you want or need, it's still a wonderful gift. Enjoy everything. Throughout my chemotherapy treatments, I was still happy to be alive. I was grateful that I could remain strong throughout my illness. Although I didn't feel my strongest on the treatment days, I was grateful to bounce back to myself on the days following treatment. With faith, determination, inner strength, and patience, I knew there would be better days ahead.

Mission: Be thankful every day for your beautiful life. Be thankful that you're alive and you can experience all of life's wonders.

August 4

■ ■ ■

Everything created is meant for change. Remain grateful, yet unattached.

There are so many things in your life to be grateful for. So many things to love and adore. If you can love, you can also lose. It's important to remain unattached to everything that you love and adore. There is a difference in loving and being attached and loving and remaining unattached. You shouldn't live your life with the feeling that you cannot live without something. It's not healthy. However, this does not mean you cannot love with all your heart.

Mission: Know that everything changes. Don't live your life being attached to an outcome of a situation. Do live with a grateful heart, no matter how long or short a time you have with those things and people you love.

August 5

▪ ▪ ▪

Everyone needs their own time. Treasure this time with yourself, it leads you back to wholeness.

If you don't take care of yourself, no one else will. Find the time to do the things you need to do to replenish your spirit, whatever they may be.

Mission: Find the time in each new day to do something that calms your mind, relaxes your body, and nourishes your soul.

August 6

▪ ▪ ▪

Don't become obsessed with anything that gets you nowhere.

Put your energy into things that fulfill your mind and spirit. Wasting time on things that get you nowhere will eventually lead to a life of frustration. You are worthy of more.

Mission: Put your focus towards the things that bring your life meaning. Life is a precious and limited gift. Use it wisely.

August 7

▪ ▪ ▪

Living in connection with your mind, body and spirit is quality living. Focusing only on one will not keep you in balance.

It takes effort to keep proper balance in check. You cannot expect to achieve balance if you only pay attention to one part of yourself. Strengthen each of the things that make up who you are.

Mission: Do something for your mind by reading books or by learning something new. Do something for your body by exercising daily. Do something for your spirit with meditation and prayer.

August 8

■ ■ ■

It's so important to be yourself. If people don't like you because of it, don't worry about it. It's better than putting on an act.

The world has so many kinds of people in it, with many different personalities. There are going to be people that just won't like you, and that's okay. You weren't meant to be everyone's best friend. You shouldn't have to try and please someone that doesn't like you. Remain yourself. It shouldn't matter who likes you or who doesn't. As long as you're not hurting anyone, then it's not your problem.

Mission: Be true to you. Avoid people and situations that make you feel "less than," or that make you feel that you must be someone other than yourself. Stay with those who love your company, lift your spirit, and are easy to be with. Good relationships should never be a chore.

August 9

■ ■ ■

Everyone needs something to believe in. Begin with yourself.

It can be difficult to go through life without faith in something. Believing in a higher power (God) helps us to realize that there is more to this life, especially when things get tough. Keeping a belief in oneself is necessary. You need to have strength, courage, and self -confidence to get through life.

Mission: Ask yourself what your beliefs are. Whom do you turn to when life gets tough? Whom do you trust? Ask yourself these questions. The answers may change your perception.

August 10

▪ ▪ ▪

Never allow someone to take away the person you are. If there is someone in your life that wants to change you, then maybe they don't belong in your life.

Everyone deserves freedom to be themselves. You should never have to be anyone other than you. You are always enough. You are always worthy of goodness. You should never feel forced to change for anyone else's sake.

Mission: Re-evaluate your relationships. If someone doesn't add value to your life, or pressures you to be someone other than yourself, it may be time to move on from them.

August 11

■ ■ ■

Nothing comes easy. Everything earned takes work. It's the journey that matters most, not the destination.

Hard work usually pays off. If there's something you're going after, give it your all. A little hard work never hurt anyone. Anything worthwhile never comes easy.

Mission: Find what you love to do. Let your passion lead the way towards greatness.

August 12

■ ■ ■

A positive mind will eventually lead to a positive life.

A positive outlook changes everything. It can turn a hopeless situation into a hopeful one. The power of positivity isn't fake. It's a real force that can change your perception when you practice positive thinking.

Mission: *Try seeing every negative situation as a positive lesson.*

August 13

■ ■ ■

Never assume something just from the looks of it, whether it be a person, situation, or piece of gossip.

Nothing in life is as it seems and assumptions are not usually accurate. The best way to know anything for sure is to ask.

Mission: Beginning today, make a point to find out the facts. Ask questions so you'll know the answers. Stop assuming the reasons for things that you're unsure of.

August 14

▪ ▪ ▪

The best thing about being you is that no one else can be, no matter how hard they try.

It's a great feeling to be unique. Each person has something all their own. Be grateful that you cannot be duplicated. You are a special gift to the world.

Mission: Aim to be the best version of yourself every day. Be better than you were yesterday.

August 15

■ ■ ■

Sometimes you need to lose yourself in order to find yourself again.

Life can get tough at times. Changes happen that you don't expect and you may feel like a lost soul. When I was diagnosed with cancer, I felt this way. But deep down in my heart I knew I'd find my way again. Though I had to dig deep, I wouldn't let it get the best of me. I wasn't going to let the disease change the person I was, no matter what the doctors were saying. Don't get me wrong, it was quite a scary time, and it still is. I never wanted to let the disease define the person I am, I am so much more. It's just something that happened to me. I had to learn to expect the unexpected. I realized that my hardships would only make me stronger.

Mission: Never lose hope for better days. They will always be on their way.

August 16

■ ■ ■

Those who are unhappy tend to criticize those who are happy.

Unhappy people don't always see the good that's in front of them. If they can't see goodness in their own life, they won't care to see it in anyone else's.

Mission: Take notice of those unhappy people in your life. Try to understand the reason they act as they do. Help them learn to be grateful for the things they take for granted.

August 17

▪ ▪ ▪

Sensitivity towards others shows that you are human, not weak.

The world needs more sensitive people. Life can be tough sometimes. We need to show support by being empathetic towards one another. By showing others you care, you're making the world a better place.

Mission: *Give someone your support today.*

August 18

▪ ▪ ▪

It's important to believe that the universe is on your side. There is a plan for you in the works right now, to your benefit.

Everything comes down to what you believe. If you truly believe that the universe (God), is there for you, that is what you will find. If you go through life as a non-believer, it's more difficult to get through tough times. There needs to be a meaning to your life. Without belief, there is none.

Mission: Learn to be a believer. Good things come to those who believe.

August 19

■ ■ ■

Everything you do that brings you presently in the moment is done most perfectly.

When you live in the moment, you are in charge of that moment. If you're constantly distracted by thoughts, you'll never live presently. You'll never enjoy what's in front of you at the time. Being in the moment brings you the most joy and fulfillment.

Mission: Be present in all you do today.

August 20

■ ■ ■

Never put your trust in someone who doesn't trust himself.

When people don't trust themselves, they cannot be considered trustworthy.
It takes time and experience to truly trust yourself, though it should be attained. It's important for living.

Mission: Learn to trust yourself before anyone else. Be selective when placing your trust in others.

August 21

▪ ▪ ▪

If you choose to give up, then change can never happen.

Many people seem to give up just as they are getting closer to their goal. Keep walking through your obstacles. If you've come half-way, then you can go to the end. Challenges bring change.

Mission: Don't get discouraged so easily. Give yourself the chance to make a change for the better.

August 22

▪ ▪ ▪

Your time is NOW. Don't waste another day focusing on something that doesn't bring you closer to your purpose.

Living your purpose is what life is all about. It may take a half a lifetime to figure it out, but it's worth it. You are here for a reason. Maybe it's to be a blessing for someone else. Keep searching for your purpose. Begin with recognizing what brings joy to your spirit.

Mission: *Today, write down all the things you plan to accomplish. Begin taking the necessary steps towards making your life, your purpose.*

August 23

▪ ▪ ▪

Only you have the power to make every day a worthwhile one.

You have the power to do anything you want. You can design a life you've dreamed about. It's all within you. You can do anything you set your mind to.

Mission: When you wake up each morning, set your sights on the things that bring you joy, then do more of that.

August 24

▪ ▪ ▪

Your habits will eventually become your lessons, whether good or bad.

What a person does with their time says a lot about them. Make sure you're on a good path. Don't be a follower. Stay true to yourself by following your own heart.

Mission: Become aware of your daily habits. Try to undo the bad ones that don't serve you well. Replace them with better ones that resonate with your heart and are beneficial to your life.

August 25

▪ ▪ ▪

Never lose sight of your dreams, they are what keep your spirit alive.

Your dreams form your future. It's important to keep striving to attain your goals no matter what obstacles you're confronted with. When your dream dies, so will your spirit. Stay on course or find a better one.

Mission: *Make it a point to become aware every day of how you want your life to unfold. Be led by your spirit. Keep your dreams alive.*

August 26

▪ ▪ ▪

Creativity can be hindered or brought to higher heights. Make sure you're not wasting yours by staying idle or settling for a life that's mediocre.

You weren't meant to have an average life. You were meant to progress to your highest self. This takes some work but it can be done. Wherever you are in your life right now, choose to progress one step further.

Mission: *Share your talents today and every day. They weren't meant to be kept hidden inside of you. You were blessed with them for a reason.*

August 27

■ ■ ■

If ever you feel the need to compromise your character for the sake of others, then you're hanging with the wrong crowd.

If you should decide to follow what doesn't feel right in your heart, you'll be led down the wrong path. Temptation is sometimes difficult to turn away, but it's a necessity to steer clear from detours that will not suit your purpose.

Mission: There should never be a time for you to act other than yourself. Be confident in the person you are every day. Listen to yourself.

August 28

■ ■ ■

No matter how positive an attitude you maintain, there will always be some negativity in your way.

Your attitude affects all areas of your life. When you can't seem to avoid negativity, remain quiet and realize that those who are this way haven't found peace in their own life. Don't take it personal, it's not even about you.

Mission: *Take no insult from others. No matter what obstacles appear in front of you, see the positive.*

August 29

■ ■ ■

With every change comes new possibilities. Learn to embrace change, not resist it. From there, you can learn more about yourself and your infinite potential.

Many people fear change, not realizing that change is growth. Throughout life there will be many changes. Nothing in life stays the same forever.

Mission: *Learn to become comfortable with changes in your life. Go with them, they may lead to greater things.*

August 30

▪ ▪ ▪

Temperature is crucial for keeping a perfect balance. Keep your manner mild, your attitude cool and your heart warm.

A balanced life is a good life. Take the time to give necessary attention to each area of your life. Don't focus too much on one thing.

Mission: *Beginning today, keep everything you do in balance. It's the key to living a calm, happy life.*

August 31

■ ■ ■

Once you stop being afraid to be who you are, you'll find that the world will want you no other way.

Every day of your life should leave you a step closer to who you were meant to be. Be proud of who you've become so far. Stay eager to take on new challenges, dare to be different and stay confident in the person you are.

Mission: Let your confidence lead the way today. Be authentic!

September

September 1

▪ ▪ ▪

You don't need anyone to complete you. You are already complete. Finding your purpose in life will enhance your completeness.

Many people go through life trying to find someone who "completes" them. I believe the word is complement. Finding someone who complements the person you are is the best thing you can hope to find.

Mission: If you're feeling incomplete, look for hobbies and things that make you feel whole. Remember, it's not in another person that you'll find this. It's within yourself that leads to wholeness.

September 2

▪ ▪ ▪

When you can say that you are your own best friend, then you are the luckiest person in the world.

Enjoying your own company is the best feeling in the world. It's liberating, uplifting and you'll never be lonely.

Mission: Today, instead of going somewhere with a friend, try going alone. Learn to become comfortable doing something alone, learn to love YOU.

September 3

■ ■ ■

The more peace you bring to others, the more peaceful you'll become.

The world needs more peacemakers. Living life brings a lot of tension and sometimes trouble. Avoid trouble and help others steer clear of it by keeping a sense of calm about yourself. In turn, you will bring that same sense to all you encounter.

Mission: *Be the peacemaker. Be the calm to someone's storm.*

September 4

■ ■ ■

Sometimes you'll need to travel down a dark and gloomy road in order to get to the gloriously bright one.

Life is inconsistent, it has its ups and downs. When you go through difficult times, you're being prepared for something great that is yet to come.

Mission: Today, stop and realize that all difficult times will come to pass and you will become a better and stronger person for it.

September 5

■ ■ ■

When others try to control your decision making, your plans, or your life, then they aren't meant for you. No person should control another, no matter who they are.

Your life is your own. You should never feel the pressure of having to listen to another if your heart isn't for it.

Mission: *Re-evaluate the people you choose to have in your life. Ask yourself if they bring out your best or if they put a damper on your spirit.*

September 6

▪ ▪ ▪

Always keep faith and hope in your heart. Losing your faith is like going skydiving without a parachute.

Without faith and hope, you are shortchanging yourself. Having faith and a hopeful mind will set your life in the right direction. Without it, you'll have no chance to make anything right.

Mission: Keep a hopeful spirit all through your life. Believing in a higher power that guides you along life's path is essential. You are never alone.

September 7

■ ■ ■

Each time you move out of your comfort zone you're moving closer to a more confident self.

Sometimes you must do things that absolutely terrify you in order to progress. Everyone has something that frightens them, but that may be the very thing that you need to do.

Mission: *Never stop learning and growing, even if it takes some courage. Every new change becomes growth in yourself. Seek new knowledge and opportunity in every new day.*

September 8

■ ■ ■

Once you realize what you're here to do, the universe will help see you through.

When you have a clear vision of your purpose and take action each day towards making it happen, you will find that more amazing opportunities will come to you. Doors will open for you, and the right people will show up.

Mission: *Find those things that you enjoy. This will lead you on the path to your purpose.*

September 9

■ ■ ■

A life lived in fear is no life at all. The next time you're overpowered by fear, remember that your mind has created that fear and your mind can take it away. Don't let it get the best of you.

Many times, fear gets in the way with our future goals. If we don't get past them, we'll always be in the same place.

Mission: *Take one step to get past your fear today. Remember that you're in control.*

September 10

■ ■ ■

Pay attention to NOW. Be with it, live in it and never take it for granted. It's your present.

Live presently. Whatever it is that you're doing will be your absolute best. Right now, is the only moment of importance. It's the only time that is real. There is no other time in your life that is guaranteed.

Mission: *Make a habit of staying in the moment with everything you do daily. Stop racing through your day.*

September 11

■ ■ ■

You should never feel too cool to be kind. You must be cool to be kind.

Kindness is a mentality. It's something you should carry within your heart and mind each day. Whomever you meet will be blessed with your kind spirit.

Mission: Let random acts of kindness become a part of your daily routine.

September 12

▪ ▪ ▪

A lack of progression can kill your spirit. Enhance your creativity by doing the things that are of interest to you.

Too many times we stop and settle when things get challenging. You have too much potential to settle for mediocre. You must continually use your gifts and talents each day. They will take you where you're meant to be.

Mission: Make it a point to keep moving forward. Practice doing what you love to do and get better at it.

September 13

■ ■ ■

As long as you maintain the ability to give, you will remain a blessing.

What is the reason for living but not giving? There's nothing good in hoarding all your blessings. Bless others with your gifts. They were meant to be shared.

Mission: *Today, give something away to someone who needs it. There's no greater feeling than giving.*

September 14

▪ ▪ ▪

When you've learned to find peace within yourself, there is nothing that can shake you.

All your lessons are learned through experience. They will make you stronger, wiser, and hopefully a more peaceful spirit. The more you experience, the stronger you'll become. Be thankful for your lessons.

Mission: *Today, give yourself 15 minutes of alone time. Sit quietly and feel all your feelings. Meditate on all the good in your life. Be grateful for it, and you will bring more of it.*

September 15

■ ■ ■

Expect the most from yourself, not others. You are a powerful being. Once you start believing that way then you will start living that way.

Your mind is your most powerful tool. Be careful of your inner dialogue, it sets the tone for the day.

Mission: *Realize that you are capable of accomplishing anything you set your mind to. Practice being patient with yourself.*

September 16

■ ■ ■

The desire for things to be better is the first step in getting them that way.

Desire is the seed that begins to grow within the spirit when you want something badly enough. Follow that. Desire is what you need first to attain anything. It's the first step towards success.

Mission: *Envision whatever it is you want out of life. Make a point to consistently think about it. Become obsessed with it. Then take small steps towards it.*

September 17

■ ■ ■

Everything in life changes. Circumstances change, people change and landscapes change. You can't dodge change, just learn to move with it.

Change can be very positive. When we are forced to change something, we will see it in a new light. Wherever there is change, there is newness. Consider all changes a time for progression.

Mission: Today, make some room for growth in all areas of your life. Learn to look at change as something positive and good.

September 18

■ ■ ■

Sometimes you must figure out what you don't want in order to get what you want.

When you learn to eliminate the negatives that are in your life then you can make the way for positives. Try to do away with as much stress and negativity as possible. Accept the things that cannot be changed.

Mission: *Write down all the things you do not want in your life. Make a clear path for all the things that you do want.*

September 19

▪ ▪ ▪

Cherish everything that matters to you and don't take anything for granted. Keep your life meaningful.

Be thankful every day for those things that add value and meaning to your life. Imagine life without those things. Be sure to nourish all that is good in your life by giving proper attention and care. Honor them.

Mission: Each day, appreciate all that you have and all that is on its way to you.

September 20

■ ■ ■

Loving and accepting yourself is just as important as exercising your body. It takes time and consistency to develop.

It takes time to love and accept yourself as you are. It can sometimes take half your lifetime to be comfortable in your own skin. It's something that needs to be practiced every day.

Mission: Do something today that makes you feel good about yourself. Learn to treat yourself with care.

September 21

■ ■ ■

You are remarkable and capable of anything you set out to do. Don't doubt your abilities. Life is too short. Just go for it!

Everything you desire begins with the mind. First, you'll need to believe the things you tell yourself. Then get the first step started. Don't put off till tomorrow the things that can be done today.

Mission: *Make something happen today. Stop procrastinating!*

September 22

■ ■ ■

No matter what's going on in your life, whether there's chaos, sadness, confusion, or darkness, choose to focus on the positive things that you have. Train your mind on seeing the good.

Whatever we choose to focus on will bring just that. Be aware of your thoughts. Recall happy, joyful thoughts. Be grateful for all the goodness in your life. Good thoughts bring good things. Make this your mindset.

Mission: Find peace and appreciation in those positive things in your life, however small.

September 23

▪ ▪ ▪

Don't expect to have laughter if you make others miserable. Don't expect to be loved if all you do is criticize. Don't expect to have peace if all you promote is chaos. Don't expect a change if you haven't done anything different. Don't expect to receive from anyone what you cannot give to yourself.

It's plain and simple, you get what you give.

Mission: *Do unto others as you'd have done to you. Remember too, whatever you give, you get. Promote a kinder world.*

September 24

■ ■ ■

The things you take for granted will always be the best things you'll ever have.

The simplest things in life are most overlooked. Your family and friends, your work, your health, your abilities, to name a few. These are precious commodities. If you didn't have them, where would you be?

Mission: *Take care of all the things that make your life better and easier. Let all those special people in your life know how much they are appreciated.*

September 25

■ ■ ■

Be thankful that you can be thankful.

You are lucky when you can be thankful for something. I believe we all can be. Take notice of all those things in your day to be thankful for. It can be anything from your cup of morning coffee to the car that brings you to work.

Mission: Look around you today and see all the beauty there is in your life, in your home and in your heart, and be thankful.

September 26

▪ ▪ ▪

It is when you have learned to love, forgive, and stay peaceful, that you will be treasured.

Love, forgiveness, and peace are not so freely given, and they don't come easy. When you can find these three qualities in yourself or find them in another, you have found a treasure.

Mission: Always work on bettering yourself. Compete with the person you were yesterday, and keep striving to become a gem.

September 27

■ ■ ■

It's important to stay both interesting and interested. Interesting enough to teach and interested enough to learn.

Everyone admires someone knowledgeable. Knowing a little something about everything is being well rounded, and that's a good thing. Read the newspaper, talk to those who are knowledgeable, and keep your mind open. Expanding your mind can open new doors for you. Knowing you can have a conversation with anyone is an asset.

Mission: Stay eager to learn and eager to teach. It's what makes your life worth living for yourself and others.

September 28

■ ■ ■

The world can be chaotic. Choose to be a peacemaker and make the world a better place. It begins with YOU!

Keep the peace wherever you go. More people will long to be around you as your presence will have a calming effect. Practice this until it becomes second nature.

Mission: *Steer clear of drama. It's unnecessary, it's draining and it serves no purpose.*

September 29

■ ■ ■

When you doubt your worth, you'll wind up settling for less. Always believe you are deserving of more.

When you settle for less, you are shortchanging yourself and your life will be limited. You are worthy of so much more than you know.

Mission: *Wake up every day believing that the world is your oyster. You will always have more than enough.*

September 30

■ ■ ■

The most important thing to learn to carry the right way is yourself.

You have one life. Live with dignity, courage, respect, class, and self- confidence. Rely mostly on yourself and always, always, always, live with a grateful heart.

Mission: Respect yourself and respect those around you. Try to earn the respect of those that are respected.

October

October 1

■ ■ ■

Being yourself should be the easiest thing to do. It should never feel like a struggle. You should never feel that you must prove something to anyone.

You were blessed to be given this life. Staying true to you is the best way to live it. It will sometimes drag you down, but don't give in. Get back up. Keep getting better and stronger.

Mission: *Appreciate who you've become, but keep striving to be better. Stay challenged and prove things to yourself. There's no one else that could take the place of YOU.*

October 2

■ ■ ■

To bring out the best in others, you should help them believe in their own potential.

It's important to give credit where it's due. Don't hold back paying a compliment on how well someone has done something. Many people could use a pat on the back now and then to make them feel good about themselves.

Mission: Give someone a compliment today. Let them know something about themselves that makes them special. Be a confidence builder.

October 3

■ ■ ■

Criticizing others only shows your own insecurities.

Most people aren't aware that when they show criticism towards others, it's their own insecurities being projected. Help the betterment of others by seeing the positives in their character and making it known.

Mission: *Make a habit of seeing the good in others. Let someone know that they're doing a great job.*

October 4

■ ■ ■

Be confident and steadfast in your beliefs. It builds character and helps to earn the trust of others.

A confident and steadfast character is a trustworthy one. It shows diligence, heart, passion, and care. Staying consistently confident in all that you do makes you admirable. It shows you mean what you say. People will trust you.

Mission: Make a point to follow through with the things you say you're going to do. Become someone who is reliable. Be an example.

October 5

■ ■ ■

Do whatever you can while you still can!

Life is meant to be lived. Don't put things off to the future. You never know what the future may bring. Live life each day to the fullest.

Mission: Keep the mentality that life is short. Do what you want to do. Live NOW!

October 6

■ ■ ■

Worrying always makes matters worse and most things aren't worth it.

Worrying can take a lot of your energy. It's depleting, yet gets you no where, except down. It's damaging to the soul. Give hope a chance instead. You can always find hope in a hopeless situation, tap into your higher conscience. Remember, without storms there wouldn't be rainbows.

Mission: *Stop stressing. Put your trust in a higher power, get some exercise and just breathe.*

October 7

■ ■ ■

Whatever you do, do with grace and integrity.

It's not always easy to do the right thing in life, but it should always be a priority.

Mission: Don't lose yourself when problems arise. Pay attention to what's right. Always do the best that you can in any situation, whether good or bad.

October 8

■ ■ ■

The world will never be exactly how you want it to be, but each of us has the ability to make one small change to make it a better place.

If you want to see a change for the better in the world, begin with yourself. Yes, it's as simple as that. Work on being a better person. Try having more compassion for those less fortunate. Try to imagine yourself in someone else's shoes before you pass judgment. Don't doubt that you, alone, can make the world a better place.

Mission: *Teach kindness to others by your words and actions. Live your life as an example for others.*

October 9

■ ■ ■

The greatest gift you can give someone is acceptance of who they are with no judgments, just unlimited understanding, and love.

Everyone needs acceptance. To be free to be who you are is sacred. Acceptance of self helps you to go through life without the worry of judgment from others. Be free to be you and offer the same to others.

Mission: *Today, try to have more patience with the difficult people in your life. Accept them for who they are.*

October 10

■ ■ ■

There are only so many times you can travel down the same road without changing the person you are. Wisdom is gained through experiences.

You cannot travel down the same intricate road over and over, yet keep a simple mind. Life's trials bring strength to your psyche. Your mindset changes, which makes you aware that you are not in charge of every aspect of your life. There is a guiding, divine force behind the scenes.

Mission: Have faith in the divine force in your life. It's there to help you, not hurt you.

October 11

■ ■ ■

Kindness... never take it for granted, always receive it as a blessing, never mistake it for stupidity or weakness, and always return it.

The world could always use a little more kindness. Be someone who believes in the power of a kind word, kind act, and a giving heart. There is no one that can't use a little more kindness in their life.

Mission: *Show kindness to someone who needs it today.*

October 12

▪ ▪ ▪

Every one of you has something within that has the desire to become better than yesterday. The desire to evolve into the best person you can be is in there, follow it!

Progression is the key to fulfillment in life. You are meant to be so much more than the person you are now. You were meant to progress to your best self. Stop doubting the fact that you're worthy.

Mission: Make it a point to progress from where you are at this point in your life. Aim to be better than yesterday. Do something more, however small.

October 13

■ ■ ■

Inspiration can come when you least expect it. Always keep an open heart and mind.

Everyone can find something or someone that inspires them. Sometimes it's necessary in order go a step further. Inspiration can be just the motivation you need to become something more. It's a great feeling to find inspiration. It can be like the wind beneath your wings.

Mission: *Find something or someone that inspires you. Even better, become an inspiration to others.*

October 14

■ ■ ■

The key to happiness is getting over yourself and connecting with others. True happiness comes when you give to others whatever it is that you want for yourself.

When you learn to give, you'll live a better life as a better person. Your life will become more satisfying as "the giver". When you focus on others' needs you will feel better about yourself. It's a fact that givers are happier people than takers. Life doesn't revolve around you.

Mission: Today, give something that you would love to have for yourself, to someone else.

October 15

■ ■ ■

Nothing in life is overly complicated until the mind gets involved.

Whenever you overthink a situation, it becomes worse. Sometimes you'll need to let things happen as they will. Realize that everything is not in your control. Once you can accept this fact, the more peaceful a person you'll become. Remember, things have a way of working themselves out.

Mission: *Stop overthinking things. It causes unnecessary worry and complications. Learn to let it go. Take things as they come and just roll with them.*

October 16

■ ■ ■

Sometimes it's your mistakes that keep you humble, grounded, and on the right track.

To be human is to make mistakes. No one is perfect, nor will they ever be. The only thing that you can try to perfect is your attitude. Your attitude should be worked on daily, until it becomes your greatest asset. This is how you'll progress as a person. It can make you or break you.

Mission; *Learn from every experience. Pay attention to what each experience teaches, then apply it in your life.*

October 17

■ ■ ■

It's only when you stop giving that you'll begin lacking.

When you learn to live with a giving heart, your world becomes more abundant. Give to those less fortunate, care for those in need. Go out of your way to show others that you care. This is what life is all about. This way of living enhances everyone involved, both giver and receiver.

Mission: Reach out to someone today. Try to make it a daily practice.

October 18

▪ ▪ ▪

Whatever makes your spirit dance and your heart sing is worth your while.

It's not that difficult to find your passion in life. When you listen to you heart, you'll know what brings you joy, and you'll do it best. This is one of the most important things you can do for yourself

Mission: Find what you love to do. Then find the time to incorporate it into your schedule.

October 19

■ ■ ■

Peace and contentment comes when you accept that you are exactly where you're supposed to be.

Each moment of your life is precious. Each moment of your life is meant to unfold just the way it is. Don't rush it away and don't beg it to stay. Just be here, right now. It's part of your journey, whether painful or pleasurable.

Mission: Learn to trust that everything that's happening to you right now is supposed to be.

October 20

▪ ▪ ▪

It is your right and your responsibility to express your full potential.

Each new day is a chance to live out your dreams. Stop downplaying your abilities. You have unlimited potential. Everything you are capable of begins in your mind first. Once it's there, the body will follow.

Mission: Realize your power to excel. Don't ever hold back or feel guilty for being your best. Claim it!

October 21

■ ■ ■

Don't try to look like a winner on someone else's expense. Everyone has moments when they aren't at their best. You'll never shine if you point out the weakness of another in order to look better.

Putting others down will never make you look better in the long run. It's always better to speak highly of others or say nothing at all. Remember, the things you say about others reflects a lot about you.

Mission: *Get in a habit of raising up others.*

October 22

■ ■ ■

Live better, aim higher, work smarter, and most of all, love more abundantly.

It's important to live with abundance in your heart. Let abundance flow through all areas of your life.

Mission: Give your all every day, even when things are not going well.

October 23

■ ■ ■

It is when you learn not to expect from, or attach yourself to anyone or anything, that you will never be disappointed.

Your life depends on YOU. Your decisions, your words and actions, your everything. There will be times you'll need some help along the way, but don't depend on it for the long haul.

Mission: Learn to love all things without forming attachment to them.

October 24

▪ ▪ ▪

If you keep saying NO to life, then life will keep saying NO back.

You can have anything you want with the right mindset. Sometimes a change in perception is necessary. Say yes to new opportunities that come your way. You must be open to change and newness in order to move forward.

Mission: Open your eyes and heart to new beginnings and new challenges. Say yes to change.

October 25

■ ■ ■

Don't cheat or shortchange yourself. Your life is your own. You deserve more than you know.

Only you know the path you've journeyed along. Only you know how strong you've become from trials and tribulations. Expecting good things to come your way is a step in the right direction. It's time to accept all the goodness you deserve.

Mission: *Go after everything you've ever wanted without holding back. Live without limits and realize that you can have it all if you believe you can.*

October 26

■ ■ ■

With every obstacle placed in your way, hurdle over it with hope. With every thought of uncertainty, think through it with hope. With every fear of the unknown, conquer it with hope. With every question unanswered, hope is the answer.

Where there is hope, there is always a way to make things better. Living with a hopeful spirit helps you to realize that things can turn around. Unfortunate situations don't have to stay that way when there is hope in your heart and mind. Being hopeful can cause miracles to happen in your life.

Mission: *Live with a hopeful spirit every day. Practice thinking with hope in mind.*

October 27

■ ■ ■

Not stepping out of your comfort zone is like never leaving your house.

To reach higher heights, you need to get uncomfortable. You need to take some chances, get a little bolder, believe in yourself a little more. Trusting yourself is the most important thing you can do to get a little further from where you are now.

Mission: *Today, try something that you've always wanted to do, but never had the courage.*

October 28

■ ■ ■

Give yourself permission to fail. Nothing great will ever be attempted or accomplished if you do not leave room for error.

It's not a perfect world, nor will it ever be, but we can't give up. We need to accept our mistakes and realize that our mistakes are what bring us to success. Without mistakes, we wouldn't gain the wisdom and the insight to become successful.

Mission: *Ask yourself the question, "What's the worst that can happen if I fail?" This will make it easier to live according to your best ability, not to the standard of perfection. Know in your heart that you will get to where you need to be if you keep the right attitude.*

October 29

▪ ▪ ▪

Never allow yourself to lose the capacity for joy. Consciously choose to create it.

Nothing should keep you down. Whatever may be going on in your life at this time will pass, as nothing good or bad remains constant. Keep moving forward as you fill your mind with good thoughts and feelings.

Mission: *Look for joy in the simplest things.*

October 30

■ ■ ■

Your world is a reflection of your thoughts.

Your thoughts can steer you in a good or bad direction. Keeping your thoughts on a positive note is key for bringing positive things, events, and people your way. Even though you cannot control everything that goes on in your life, you can always try your best to keep a positive mindset. If negative thoughts arise in your mind, quickly change them to something better.

Mission: Re-train your brain to think only positive things and dismiss the negatives. Practice this daily.

October 31

■ ■ ■

Keep everything that's made you happy, in your heart. Think of them often, when your days aren't as bright. For these are the memories which will help you realize that everything will be all right again.

Making memories is something everyone should do on a regular basis. Continue to plan things to look forward to. Keep building memories. One day as you look back on your life, you'll know that you've lived, loved, and shared some good times throughout your lifetime. They're proof that you've lived a good life.

Mission: Make a point to reflect on those good times you've had in life, and the people you've enjoyed spending time with. Keep your memories in your heart.

November

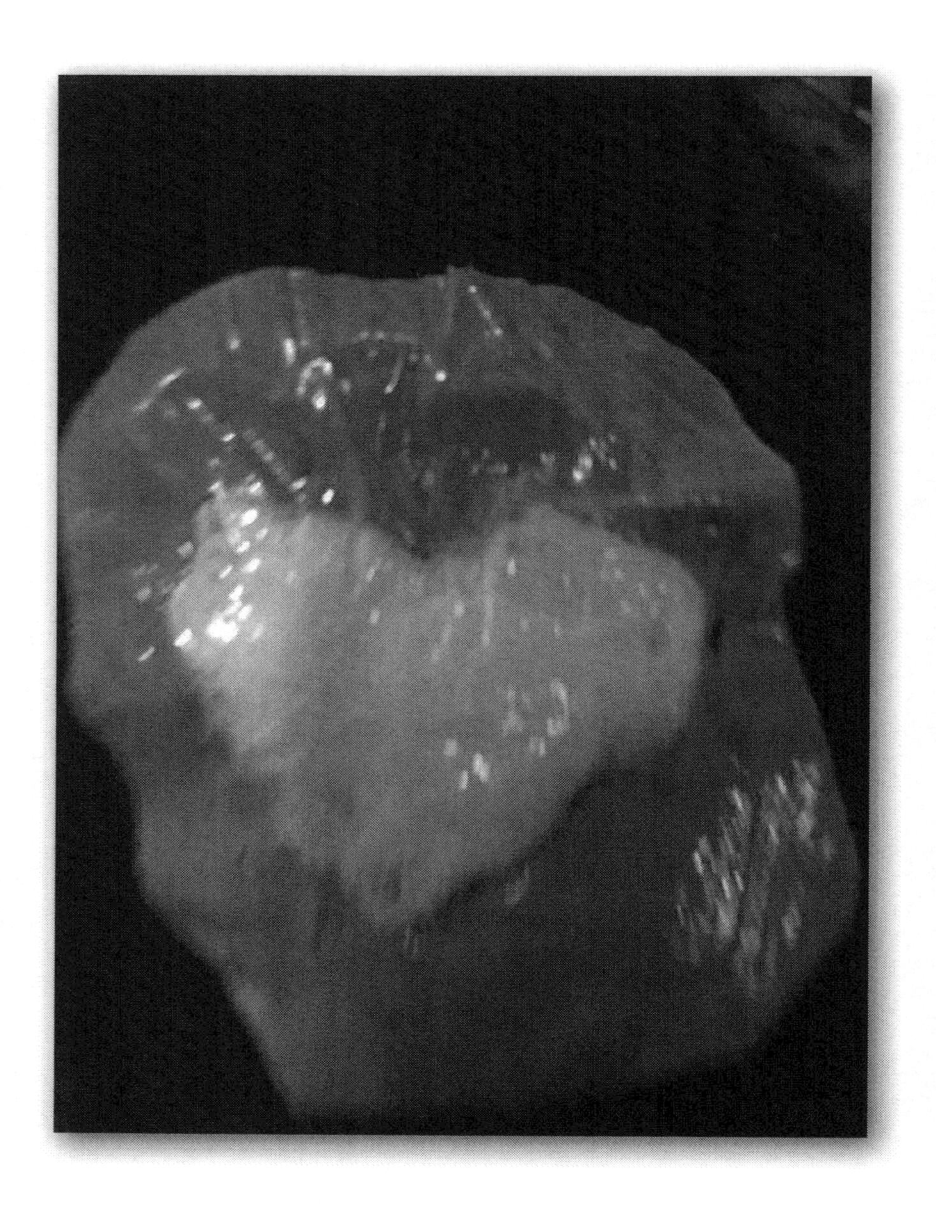

November 1

▪ ▪ ▪

You can't give what you don't have, you'll never become someone you're not intended to be, and you'll never master what isn't practiced.

As time goes on you'll realize your capabilities. When you put your focus and intention into something, whether it be your career or your hobby, you'll find that you'll get better at it. When you find the thing you love to do, keep doing it. Find whatever it is that makes your life worth living.

Mission: *Stay diligent with your work and aware in your mind regarding your life's path.*

November 2

▪ ▪ ▪

Sometimes those things we think are so far-fetched, are really at close range.

Nothing is as impossible as it seems. You must live your life with an unwavering faith and belief in yourself that all dreams can be accomplished. Forty- four percent of people that write down their dreams make them happen in reality.

Mission: *Be a do-er. Never doubt your ability to make things happen.*

November 3

▪ ▪ ▪

You have the choice every day to choose love over anger, kindness over selfishness, patience over frustration, and modesty over audacity.

Life is full of choices. Every choice you make determines the experience you'll encounter. You have the option to choose your attitude towards life, and having the right attitude can make all the difference. When you stop resisting the things that are out of your control, your life will become less of a struggle.

Mission: *Start paying attention to all the choices you make and how they affect your life.*

November 4

▪ ▪ ▪

Patience is a great virtue. It teaches discipline and confirms the fact that everything in life happens at the moment it should.

Don't feel the need to rush things. Let them move along as they should. Too many times we rush the things that are not meant to be a part of our destiny.

Mission: *Learn to be patient. If there is news you're waiting to hear, or something new you're ready to begin, stay patient, things will present themselves as they should.*

November 5

■ ■ ■

You must learn what you want to earn what you want, and when you get what you want, don't neglect what you've got.

Everything you want takes time. Sometimes just knowing what you want takes time. It won't just happen.

Mission: *Reflect on the time and energy it took to attain your goals. Realize that you can do anything you set your mind to. Then, once you receive what you want, take the necessary steps to maintain it.*

November 6

▪ ▪ ▪

Don't wait for others to celebrate you. Celebrate yourself, every day!

You shouldn't live your life waiting for others to notice you or your talents. You don't need the compliments and praise of others to know your worth. You are unique and special.

Mission: *Be proud of your accomplishments and make it a habit to reward yourself whenever possible.*

November 7

■ ■ ■

Everything you touch turns to gold. This is what you need to believe to succeed.

The power of positive thinking goes very far. Think positive thoughts about yourself daily. Self -dialogue is crucial for your success. You become what you believe yourself to be.

Mission: *Learn to tell yourself, "Yes, I can!"*

November 8

■ ■ ■

A life without visions and goals is like a highway without signs.

Your visions and goals give you a sense of direction. They structure your life. Everyone needs a set course to follow. This is the way to success.

Mission: *Decide what you want to do, where you need to go, and how long it will take you to get there.*

November 9

■ ■ ■

You can become anything you want. You can overcome any obstacle that comes your way, and you can reach any destination you choose.

You have the power to do anything you set your mind to. Once you've realized this, you will be unstoppable.

Mission: Own your power. Don't depend on luck to get you places. Everything you desire will come with proper discipline, inner strength, and determination.

November 10

■ ■ ■

If you spend most of your time thinking, then you're not doing enough. If you spend most of your time talking, then you're not listening enough, if you spend most of your time worrying, then you're not living enough. Try spending more time acting, because action is what brings results.

Time is valuable. If there is something you want to accomplish in life, you'll need to get busy. This could be anything from working your way towards a successful career, or spending quality time with loved ones.

Mission: *Pay attention to how you spend your time. Be sure to put time and energy into the things you want to accomplish, or they may never happen.*

November 11

▪ ▪ ▪

If you're always focused on negativity in yourself and others, then the beauty will go unnoticed.

Finding the best in yourself and in others, can make life more beautiful. You can turn your life around by concentrating on the good things.

Mission: *Learn to focus on the beauty that's within yourself and in others until the flaws are unnoticeable.*

November 12

■ ■ ■

You design your own life every day by the things you do, the clothes you wear, the words you say and the impressions you leave.

Everything you do in your life makes a statement. Live your life as a way of expressing yourself.

Mission: Be confident and proud in being your unique self. Show who you are and what you're about with everything you do.

November 13

▪ ▪ ▪

It's important to want success for others as well as yourself. Be happy for others when they achieve their goals.

Supporting others along their journey is what life is all about. Do whatever you can to help others attain their dreams. Showing that you're there for them and are supportive is a beautiful thing. You not only become a blessing to them, but you in turn, will be blessed.

Mission: *Congratulate someone for their accomplishments. Let them know they are admirable.*

November 14

▪ ▪ ▪

Your thoughts create your reality, so learn to be a great thinker!

Everything you think about leaves an impression on your day. Your thoughts have a direct effect on your feelings. Try to train your brain to think mostly good thoughts, your life will become better because of it.

Mission: Be choosy with your thoughts. Choose to create a happier self.

November 15

■ ■ ■

If you're strong, then teach others to conquer. If you're smart, then teach others to learn. If you're confident, then teach others to hope. If you're satisfied, then fill others with gratitude. If you're kind, then show others the way.

Sharing your gifts and talents with others is something we are meant to do here on earth. There's no reason we shouldn't help our fellow man. You were meant to help others with your knowledge and experiences.

Mission: *Help someone who is down on their luck. Help make their life easier. Let them know they are cared about.*

November 16

■ ■ ■

An eternally youthful soul is one who keeps an open mind to see things in an uncommon way. It keeps an open body in ways of fluidity and flexibility. It keeps an open spirit that is free and ready for new possibilities.

Staying open to new possibilities in all areas is the way in which good things will come to you in mind, body, and spirit.

Mission: *Try seeing the same old things differently. Try a new exercise to challenge your body. Realize your potential in body, mind, and spirit by thinking, being, and doing something different.*

November 17

■ ■ ■

Being passionate about something makes it become easy for you. Let your work be led by your passion.

The best way to find your passion in life is to ask yourself. "What gets me out of bed in the morning?" "What makes my soul feel joyful and fulfilled?" "What do I love doing so much that I would do it for free?" When you have the answer to these questions, you'll find your passion.

Mission: *Try to be excellent at something. Realize you don't have to be great at everything.*

November 18

▪ ▪ ▪

When you lead your life with a heart filled with good intentions, small miracles will always follow.

Goodness flows to goodness. It's like a magnetic field. Keeping good thoughts and intentions in mind for others, as well as yourself, will lead to better things.

Mission: *Expect only goodness to follow you in all your days. Learn to give off good vibes to others.*

November 19

■ ■ ■

Steer your day in the right direction. If it starts out the wrong way, it's up to you to change its course.

Don't depend on others to make your day better. You have the power inside of you to steer in a better direction. You are the captain of your ship!

Mission: *Try envisioning in your mind how you'd like your day to unfold. Hold those pictures in your mind and get your day going that way.*

November 20

■ ■ ■

Everyone needs to wish, to hope and to dream. You're never too old and it's never too late.

Never lose hope on a dream. Dreams are what keep us alive. They were put into our mind and heart for a reason.

Mission: *Do not put limits on yourself or your dreams. You were created to become your best self, no matter what your age. Giving up should never be an option.*

November 21

■ ■ ■

Sometimes you need to regress in order to progress.

There will be times in your life when you'll feel as if you're on a treadmill getting nowhere. Don't get discouraged. Sometimes it's necessary to feel this way to gain momentum to move forward. Don't give up. You may be closer to your goal than you realize.

Mission: Sometimes you must take a step backwards to move forward. This doesn't mean you won't get where you're trying to go, it just means there's more to learn along the way.

November 22

■ ■ ■

You can't always go with the flow with everything. Sometimes you need to listen to your inner voice. Let that be your guide.

Your ideas matter. Being passive and following the crowd will not lead you to your destiny. Keep your ideas alive by putting them into action.

Mission: *Tap into your inner voice today by sitting quietly. If there is something you're apprehensive or confused about doing, go inward, and find your answers.*

November 23

■ ■ ■

Whatever your mind focuses on will eventually become your reality.

Keep a clear vision of your goals and desires. Whatever you give attention to will usually come to fruition. Stay aware of the things you want in your life, the good things.

Mission: Pay attention to your thoughts on a daily basis. Do not focus on the negative, or things you don't want.

November 24

▪ ▪ ▪

Friends are a part of your overall health. They should bring love, warmth, positivity, and a sense of well -being. Cherish them. They're your choice.

The best thing about friends is that you get to choose them. Be sure that it never becomes an effort or a chore to have them in your life. If this should happen, then it's time to let them go. Your friends should add value to your life. They are your angels on earth.

Mission: Tell your friends how much you appreciate them today. They are your blessings.

November 25

▪ ▪ ▪

Live your life helping others to have a better one.

Helping others is a crucial part of life. With every experience, we learn something. Help others along the way with the knowledge you've gained to make their journey easier.

Mission: Learn to live a selfless life. Focusing only on yourself will never bring complete fulfillment. You must give back.

November 26

■ ■ ■

Live with a simple, appreciative spirit. Without that, nothing in this world will make you happy.

Learn to appreciate the simplest of things. Begin your day being thankful you woke up. From there, be thankful for your cup of morning coffee. Be thankful that you're able to talk to someone to share stories with. Be thankful you can enjoy simple things.

Mission: Make it a point to find joy in the simplest things in life. Be on a mission each day to find it in something.

November 27

▪ ▪ ▪

You can transform anything in your life beginning with one thing…DISCIPLINE.

Once you know what you want, set your mind to accomplishing it. Discipline is the most important trait to have in order to change anything in your life. Your mind is so powerful. If you want something badly enough, you will attain it.

Mission: *Learn to be mentally tough. Train your brain daily to stay focused and committed.*

November 28

■ ■ ■

If you've always worried about others' opinions of you, then you haven't truly been living.

It's time to stop worrying about the judgments of others. Free yourself from these chains. Live your life in a way which is best for you. Living to please everyone isn't possible. This mentality will never give you peace.

Mission: *Do your own thing regardless of what others think or say. Free yourself from the judgment of others. Just be You!*

November 29

■ ■ ■

Self- dialogue is the most important conversation you'll have every day of your life.

Whatever you tell yourself influences your day. From the moment you wake up in the morning till the moment you go to sleep at night, your inner dialogue is active. Always talk to yourself with positivity. Think and say good things. The things you tell yourself are the things you wind up believing.

Mission: *Pay attention to the way you speak to yourself. Begin your day on a positive note. Fill your mind with positive affirmations daily.*

November 30

■ ■ ■

The best gift you can give another is your understanding.

There are many people in life that feel misunderstood. Keep an open mind to others. Realize they may be struggling with particular issues. Encouragement may be just the thing they need. When you live with an understanding heart, you'll become a blessing to others.

Mission: *Lend a listening ear to someone in need. Be a blessing to someone who needs to be understood.*

December

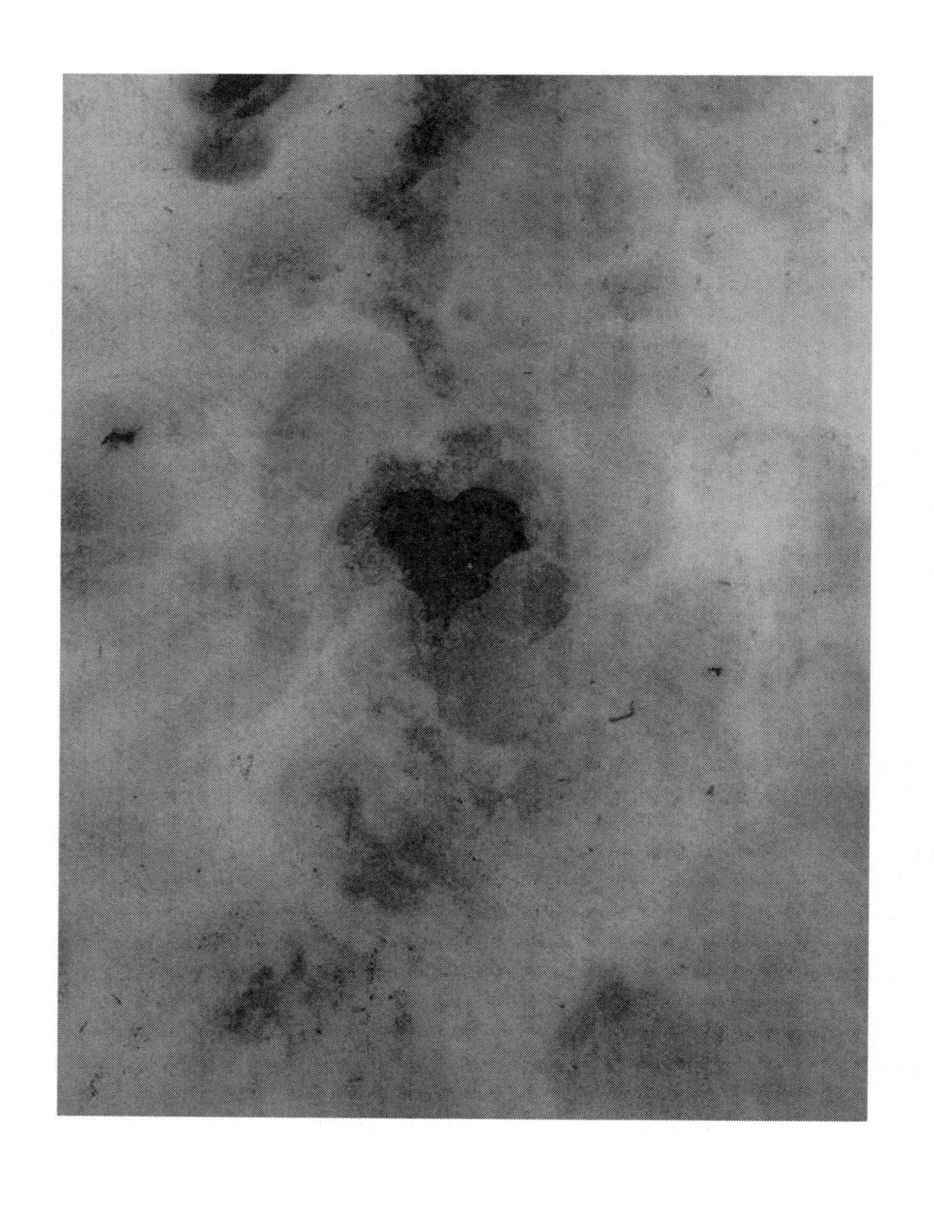

December 1

■ ■ ■

Nothing great comes easy, free, or within limits.

You cannot expect great things to fall at your feet without putting effort into it. You need to do the work. Stay diligent with your goals and they will come to you.

Mission: Keep striving for what you want and don't settle for anything less. Be bolder.

December 2

▪ ▪ ▪

When your heart is open, and you're aware of all the signs the universe reveals to you daily, then you will become more confident that there is more to this life.

There are signs that are put before you daily. Signs that you wouldn't notice unless your mind is open and aware. For instance, I have seen sightings of hearts on a daily basis. To me, this is a simple reminder that I am loved. I've included many of my heart sightings in this book, one for each month of the year. I've realized that the universe will give you everything you need when you ask.

Mission: Use your senses every day to help guide you on your path. Learn to become in tune with yourself and everything around you to bring a sense of fulfillment. Remain aware!

December 3

■ ■ ■

The day that you can say you want what you already have, is the same day that you'll realize what it means to be grateful.

Being grateful means that you are no longer searching for things you think will satisfy you and bring you happiness. Being grateful means you're already happy with what you have in your life at this time.

Mission: *Stop yourself from wanting what's not there and start appreciating what already is there. Most likely you have all that you need already.*

December 4

▪ ▪ ▪

Everyone has an effect on someone. It can be either hurtful or healing.

The effect you leave on others says a lot about the person you are. If you are encouraging with your words and inspiring in your actions, you can bring a healing power to others. If you are discouraging and critical towards others, you can leave them feeling sad and full of doubt.

Mission: Be careful of your words and behavior towards others. Choose to be a healer.

December 5

▪ ▪ ▪

Set your intention to lead a rich life. Not focusing so much on richness as in wealth, rather, aim for richness in your days. Richness in health. Richness as in making memories. Richness as in friendships along the way. These are the true riches in life.

The word "rich" goes far deeper than material items. Living a rich life means that you've touched many people. It means that you were gentle on yourself. It means that the relationships you've made have been deep. It means your days here on earth have been meaningful. It means that you were grateful for each day you were alive.

Mission: Live a meaningful life. Begin with helping one person, then another. Learn to live your life with a deeper purpose. Stop focusing so much on monetary things that will never give you a sense of fulfillment.

December 6

▪ ▪ ▪

Not everything is as great as it seems, but some things are even better than you've imagined.

Some things in life look great from a distance, but they aren't what you've expected. On the contrary, some things don't look so great but are phenomenal. It's only by experience that you would know the truth.

Mission: Believe things when you see them. It's the sure-fire way to know what's real and what's not.

December 7

■ ■ ■

Don't settle for things, choose them instead. Remember, it's your life and your choices matter.

Making the right choices in life is crucial in bringing you to the destiny you deserve. Be sure to put some thought into making important decisions. You're an important individual.

Mission: Be accountable for yourself and your life. Be selective in all areas. Envision the life that you want, then take the necessary steps to create it.

December 8

▪ ▪ ▪

You'll never fully understand why things happen in your life, just keep moving forward. It's the only direction to go.

Sometimes it's a good thing not to over analyze all the why's in life. Accept things as they come and move on from there. Don't get stuck in neutral. Even worse, do not go in reverse.

Mission: Don't get discouraged when bad things happen. Realize that there' s a bright side to every dark side that will eventually shine through.

December 9

■ ■ ■

If you spend all your time trying to fit in the crowd, you'll never realize the beauty of what makes you stand out.

Get comfortable being yourself. You are a unique individual that encompasses gifts and talents. There's never a need to fit in with a crowd. Choose to standout in the crowd. As you grow older and more confident in the person that you are, you'll want to stand out.

Mission: Keep being you, every day. You are special, you are loved and you matter. There's no one else like you in the world.

December 10

■ ■ ■

Everyone has an "aha" moment which shows just how your inner voice answers all your questions.

Once you start to trust the voice within, you will become wiser to many things. This is your guide for life.

Mission: Don't ignore your intuition. This has the answers to all of life's questions.

December 11

■ ■ ■

Nothing is impossible and everything's a miracle.

When you truly believe that nothing is impossible, your life will become amazing. You will learn to take on bigger challenges while trusting in your abilities. You will find confidence in taking that first step towards making it happen. You will become a believer. When you're a believer, miracles happen.

Mission: *Each day as you awake, think of all that you're capable of doing. Appreciate all the things presented to you in your day and see them as something special.*

December 12

■ ■ ■

When you are quick to pass judgment onto others, you not only shortchange them, but you are shortchanging yourself from what could be a beautiful friendship.

Passing judgment isn't fair. It's an unfair shortcut and an effortless way in trying to get to know someone. You can't expect others to be just like you. It's more exciting to meeting new and different minded people. The less you judge others, the more friends you'll have.

Mission: Go with the outlook of "live and let live". Different ways of others are what make life interesting. Learn from others and become diversified.

December 13

■ ■ ■

No one will ever know what you're all about until you show them what you're all about. Live your passion every day!

Let your passion lead you every day. When you are led by your passion, it shows. People will take you seriously, and look at you with confidence.

Mission: *Be sure to make yourself known to others. Share your gifts and talents as well as your hopes and dreams. They may find their inspiration from you. Be someone they aspire to become.*

December 14

■ ■ ■

Decisions decisions, they all matter. Whether it's a choice of friends, jobs, or social events, they all contribute in shaping your life. From the time you wake up until the time you end your day, the choices you make have an effect. Nothing is unimportant.

Every single decision you make, even those that seem menial, have a great impact.

Mission: *Think about all the decisions you make daily. Are they benefitting you? Try not to be hasty in your decision making. Think things through. Treat everything as though it's important, because it is!*

December 15

▪ ▪ ▪

When you speak negatively about yourself or any situation in your life, you wind up drawing more negatives towards yourself. You'll make others aware of them, even when they may not have been obvious.

It's important to focus on the positives in your life. Focusing on the positives will bring more positivity to you. When you focus on the negatives, it makes others see the negatives about you that may not have been obvious. If you begin to find positives in negative situations, you will feel happier and more in control. You will always have control of the way you perceive things.

Mission: *Don't bring attention to negativity. Always let positivity be the focus. Positive thoughts equal a positive life.*

December 16

▪ ▪ ▪

Life is a workout. Pushing off disappointments, pulling in a positive attitude, lifting others' spirits, bending some rules, and at the same time, keep things running on schedule.

It takes time and energy to keep everything in life running smoothly. Keeping your attitude positive always helps every day to be a brighter one.

Mission: *Make it a point to keep your life flowing in a positive direction. Good things happen when you have a good outlook. Life becomes magical.*

December 17

■ ■ ■

Everyone has a great moment, a great idea, and a great story, at one time or another. The more grateful you are for those times; the more greatness will come to you.

Everyone has their time to shine in life. It's important to savor those special moments. They shouldn't be taken for granted. They are your accomplishments and you've earned them. They are something to be proud of. Be grateful for them.

Mission: Wake up grateful each day. Be grateful for your bed, be grateful for the new day which you are about to embrace. Be grateful for the new opportunities it may bring. Be grateful for all you are and have yet to become.

December 18

■ ■ ■

Realizing and accepting that you can't please everyone is something that can take time. The quicker you know this the easier it will be to love yourself.

There's always going to be someone difficult in your life. Never allow that someone to leave you feeling worthless. Most likely they are projecting their own feelings onto you.

Mission: Stop trying to be the pleaser, just be yourself. Life isn't about pleasing everyone, so don't feel the need to make everyone happy, it's an impossible task.

December 19

■ ■ ■

From time to time you need to turn things around. Whether it be your direction, your attitude, or your life.

Nothing stays the same in life. You need to adjust to each change. Sometimes you'll need to begin something new. Maybe a new routine on the weekends, a different path to work, or a brand-new attitude. The same thing day in and day out can start to get old and wear you down. That's when you'll know a change is necessary.

Mission: *You'll know it's time for a change when the usual things start to feel mundane. You owe it to yourself to adapt to a new way. Keep your life exciting!*

December 20

■ ■ ■

Forgiveness cleanses the heart and soul. By allowing yourself to forgive someone, you are allowing yourself freedom.

There comes a time that you'll need to forgive. It may not be entirely for the person needing forgiveness, but for yourself as well. You cannot live the rest of your life with an unforgiving heart, you need to let it go. Then you will be free.

Mission: Stop harboring ill feelings towards someone who has done you wrong. By choosing not to forgive, you're choosing to be imprisoned.

December 21

■ ■ ■

Don't live your life under someone else's rules. Be independent. Be a leader.

You have one life. Live it the best way that you know how. Make your own decisions, enjoy your own experiences, and learn your own lessons. Your life is your own story.

Mission: Don't sell yourself short. You have the ability to make your own decisions, as this is your life. Stay in charge!

December 22

■ ■ ■

Helping others, helps you. The more you reach out to others, the clearer your purpose will become.

You all have your purpose here on earth. Sometimes you'll be unsure of what it is that you are meant to do here. Living from your heart is a great way to start.

Mission: Help someone else today. The act of giving selflessly to others is a gift from your heart.

December 23

■ ■ ■

Life can be a cold place. Never let go of those who love you, help you, and make your world a better place.

Be careful of the people you let into and out of your life. Keep the ones that lift you up and care about you. Not everyone is going to be your friend.

Mission: *Walk away from the people that don't care about you and bring you down. Show appreciation to those who matter in your life. Let them know just how much they mean to you.*

December 24

■ ■ ■

When you believe in yourself, everything flows as it should. When doubt sets in, the obstacles deter your spirit that thought it could.

Self- belief is what brings success. It enables you with the confidence you need to move forward, even with the most difficult of tasks. Never doubt your capabilities.

Mission: *Stay focused, do not allow room for doubt. Always keep a can-do attitude. There's power in believing!*

December 25

■ ■ ■

Just as you can fill your mind with positive thoughts to think, fill your mouth with positive words to say. A critical tongue cuts like a knife.

Think before you speak. If you're upset with someone at this time, don't fire out angry words. Collect yourself first, then talk things out. If you can't do that, then walk away. Sometimes words not said can be more powerful than words can say.

Mission: *Practice thoughts and words of goodness. Fill your mind with positive, uplifting thoughts. Become a creator of good things so that anyone in your presence benefits from good feelings. Let this be your gift to others.*

December 26

▪ ▪ ▪

Everything you experience in life is meant to teach you in some way. If you haven't learned or grown from a particular experience, a similar situation will reoccur.

Lessons are meant to be learned, if not, they're repeated. Take the time to learn what you need to from every experience, whether good or bad. Earth is a school and we are the students.

Mission: *Become aware of every experience you encounter. Ask yourself what it's trying to teach you. Beware of a pattern in your life that keeps bringing you to the same place.*

December 27

■ ■ ■

With everything in life, there's an opposite. With night time, comes daytime, with thunderstorms, come rainbows, with happiness, comes some darkness.

Too much of anything isn't good. Everything in life has an opposite, which brings balance. This, in turn, teaches gratitude.

Mission: Appreciate balance, without it, you'd never learn to be grateful.

December 28

■ ■ ■

Never allow yourself to become a slave, victim or fool to anything or anyone.

Respect yourself enough to live according to your own standards. You should never have to lower your standards for the sake of someone or something. This is a tell-tale sign that those things/people are not right for you.

Mission: *Learn to treat yourself well. It will set the standard on how others treat you.*

December 29

■ ■ ■

If you begin your day thinking as a pessimist, you'll surround yourself with unnecessary negative energy which already leaves you defeated.

Wake up every day and be grateful for everything in your life. When you count all those wonderful things you have, there should never be a reason to focus on negativity.

Mission: *Re-channel your way of thinking to a winning result. With optimism and positivity, you'll have a head start in the game.*

December 30

■ ■ ■

Wherever you go and whatever you do, always bring your best self with you.

Practice putting your best foot forward. Walk with confidence and spread some positive energy. You never know who may need a lift. Bring goodness everywhere you go. Help others to see themselves in a better way.

Mission: Bring goodness everywhere you go, and help others to see themselves in a better way. Spread a little love and happiness. When your heart is true, good things will follow you.

December 31

■ ■ ■

Be grateful for all the things you thought you'd never have.

Reflect on the year that has passed and keep gratitude in mind. Before you go to bed tonight and the moment you wake up in the new year's morning, choose to be grateful for everything. There was once a time you didn't have it.

Mission: Review your life and realize all the things you have that you haven't even asked for. Be thankful, for you are blessed.

Made in the USA
Middletown, DE
11 July 2017